From the Father's Heart to Yours!

Helen Jesze

Published by New Generation Publishing in 2024

Copyright © Helen Jesze 2024

First Edition

The author asserts the moral right under the Copyright, Designs and Patents Act 1988 to be identified as the author of this work.

All Rights reserved. No part of this publication may be reproduced, stored in a retrieval system or transmitted, in any form or by any means without the prior consent of the author, nor be otherwise circulated in any form of binding or cover other than that which it is published and without a similar condition being imposed on the subsequent purchaser.

ISBN

www.newgeneration-publishing.com

New Generation Publishing

King James Version KJV

© Copyright, 1957
By FRANK CHARLES THOMPSON
Entered at Stationers' Hall, London
Previous Editions
Copyright, 1908, 1917, 1929, 1934
All Rights Reserved Throughout The World

Scripture taken from the New King James Version ®. Copyright ©1982 by Thomas Nelson, Inc. Used by permission. All rights reserved.

The HOLY BIBLE, NEW INTERNATIONAL VERSION ®, NIV ®. Copyright ©1973, 1978, 1984, 2011 by Biblica,Inc. ™ Used by permission of International Bible Society ®. All rights reserved worldwide.

"Scripture taken from *THE MESSAGE.* Copyright ©1993, 1994, 1995, 1996, 2000, 2001, 2002. used by permission of NavPress Publishing Group."

"Scripture taken from THE AMPLIFIED BIBLE. Old Testament copyright ©1965, 1987 by The Zondervan Corporation. The Amplified New Testament copyright ©1958, 1987 by The Lockman Foundation. Used by permission."

"Scripture quotations are from The Holy Bible, English Standard Version ®, copyright ©2001 by Crossway, a publishing ministry of Good News Publishers. Used by permission. All rights reserved."

Bible Versions and Abbreviations

King James Version	KJV
New King James Version	NKJV
New International Version	NIV
The Amplified Bible	AMP
The Message Bible	MSG
English Standard Bible	ESV

****

Pen and Ink Sketches by Christian Artists:

Diana Fritz,	page 38
Sheena Graham,	pages 2, 10, 26
Sue Graybill	pages 18, 33, 51, 59, 61, 69

ACKNOWLEDGEMENTS

Considering *fathers,* I would first like to acknowledge my own father, Harry Richard Graham. A quiet undemonstrative man, yet I never doubted that he loved me. I thank God for his life, his prayers, the words he so often spoke from his heart – whether it was in his sermons (he was a pastor), or the words he spoke to me in everyday life.

Saved at the age of nine, my father inspired a love for God's Word in me. Each of us had a small notebook, where we wrote down how many times we had read certain books of the Bible, and the passages we had learnt by heart. We then tested each other. Dad had a great hunger for the power of the Holy Spirit in his life and would listen to Christian programs on the radio from America, as there were none at that time in England. I caught the flame in a small way and you could see us bent over the radio, late at night, trying to hear the words and music, and 'catch' the anointing of the Holy Spirit.

Together with my mother, Muriel, Dad guided me through some rocky patches in my teenage years, encouraged me in my Christian life, unconsciously mentoring me and gave me opportunity to help him in the church, and to start ministering. Messages from the 'father's heart' were invaluable.

Although not a 'father' in that sense, yet my late dear husband, George, spoke many messages from the Father's heart into my life. In almost 54 years of marriage and ministry together and apart, he continually encouraged me to follow the path which the Lord had shown me. We tried to release each other to fulfil God's calling on our lives, and I would say: Thank you George, for your love and the messages from the Father you passed on to me!

Through the years I have met many "fathers in the faith" who have spoken into my life -- encouraging, uplifting, giving wise counsel, sometimes admonishing me when necessary, praying for and standing by me, speaking from their father's heart. One of these was Bishop J.Alan Neal, pastor of Agape Christian Center in Ramstein, Germany and CEO of Elijah's Bread Ministries. We lived in Germany, and George and I belonged to this church for several years, and were greatly encouraged and supported by Bishop and his wife, First Lady Wanda.

Although we were in fulltime ministry ourselves, we always felt it was important that we belonged to a local fellowship, planted in the house of the Lord where He showed us, sitting under the ministry of the Word and having fellowship with other Christians. Bishop also opened the pulpit many times for us to minister the Word and share the prophetic. Therefore, I have asked him to write a short recommendation for this book.

Lastly and most importantly, I acknowledge my wonderful Heavenly Father, for the way He has helped and kept me through the years, for His great heart of Love and compassion, constantly reaching out to all Mankind collectively, and to each individual personally. Every one of us is so precious to Him; He sees into our heart and seeks to draw us closer to Him! Earthly fathers are not perfect; they make mistakes and are still learning themselves, but our Heavenly Father is supreme and never goes wrong, and knows just what we need! In this book, I am sharing some of the messages

from His heart in poetry and prose, and pray you will be encouraged and uplifted by them!

Helen Jesze

ENDORSEMENT

What an inspiration! My dear friend Helen Jesze's book, "From The Father's Heart To Yours," is a thought-provoking work that is the result of a life spent in the presence of our Lord and Savior Jesus – The Christ. Helen and her late husband, George, dedicated their entire lives winning souls by demonstrating the love and compassion of the Father. Her lifelong commitment to prayer, consecration, and personal devotion makes her uniquely qualified to convey these powerful messages captured in this work.

For the record, the long-term success and stability of Elijah's Bread Ministries and Agape Ministries, which comprises nearly 6000 ministries Worldwide, is due in large measure to the many prophetic utterances and words of wisdom Helen conveyed to me directly, and to my staff, helping us keep in lockstep with the heartbeat of God. As she passionately unveils the many spiritual nuggets housed within this work, my fervent prayer is that you would receive it as the Believers at Thessalonica received the Apostle Paul's words, as from "The Heart of God", and not from a mere man.

I am positive that you will find this collection of writings both comforting and encouraging. May the Lord richly bless you as you avail yourself of the many powerful messages unearthed in "From The Father's Heart to Yours."

Bishop J. Alan Neal
Presiding Bishop
Elijah's Bread Ministries &
AGAPE Ministries Worldwide

Contents

ACKNOWLEDGEMENTS v
ENDORSEMENT viii
Foreword xiv

Poems.. 1

   Grandpa and Grandma 3
   What I don't Understand 3
   Prodigal Sons and Daughters 4
   Pick up the Tools 5
   Mists in the Morning 5
   Joy comes in the Morning 6
   Harvest-Dream 7
   Cry of India! 8
   Dawn-Chorus 11
   Silent Scream 12
   Abused Restored!! 12
   After YOU, Lord, will I run!! 14
   A Trysting-Place 14
   A Garment of Praise 16
   Bird-Song 16
   Cast your Care upon Him 17
   Church on the Hill 17
   The House on the Hill 18
   Come away, my Love 19
   Come my Daughter – give me the Key! 20
   Country-Treasures 21
   Don't scratch with the Chickens 22

For such a Time!	22
For Love of Mary --- Meditation on Luke 7:36-50	23
It's the Christ of the Cross	25
To the Bride and Groom	27
Greater than All	27
Heather Country	28
He came to me	29
Holy Spirit, I'm hungry for you!	29
I refuse to worry	30
I'll be with you	31
I'm in his Hand	31
In Quietness and in Confidence	32
Laughing Jesus	33
Just the Next Step	34
Let my Heart be in your Hand	34
Live in the Now!	35
Never be a Time!	35
Out of my Way!	36
But just a Stepping-Stone	36
Let my People go!	38
See them Coming	39
Return of the Exile	40
Resting in the Lord	40
Rainbow Talk	41
Roll, roll the Stone away	41
Sometimes it seems	42
That first Easter	43
Rejoice, I'm working!	44
The Feast	45

There in your Desert 46
The Life-Mender 46
The Point of Contact 47
They're waiting... 48
This is the Day of your Favour 49
FREE! FREE! FREE! 49
To see yourself a Winner... 50
Walking through Meadow-Grass 51
Who made the Flowers 51
Wonderful Time in which to Live 52
Wrap me in your Presence 53
You're not Alone... 53
You'll still go on 54
Somebody's here 55
Under the Covering 55
After the Storm... 56
New Sunrise 57
Hold me Steady 57
Wondrous One... 58
Hiding in You 59
To Live Again! 59
The Turning-Point 60
Now Winter's here! 62

Stories in Rhyme 63

Old-fashioned Ballad of Love 64
The Farmer 65
Fisherman's Daughter... 66
Red-Shoes 68
The Vicar... 69

Ode to Pentecostals	70
The Old Man	72
The Plan	74

Inspirationals **76**

A Merry Heart!!	77
A Refuge like None Other!!	81
A Speaking God	83
An Attitude of Gratitude!	84
Behold, I will allure Her...	86
Dad's Old Saw	88
Do not remember the former Things	91
Do this, before you run!	93
Eagle Vision or *Spiritual* Vision?!	95
Forgive us our Trash-Baskets!	97
God is in Control!!	99
GOD OF THE NEW YEAR!!	100
Hands off me, you fanatic!!	103
Hey, I'm still here!!	106
I HAVE NOT FORGOTTEN YOU!!	109
It's not the End – just a new Beginning!!	112
JESUS IS THE GREATEST!! by George Jesze	115
Jesus, you have done all things well!	118
Joy and Challenge of Summer Days	120
JOY BECAUSE JESUS CAME!!	122
NEW BEGINNINGS!	124
No Black in Heaven!	126
On Wings like Eagles!!	128
Practising Pagan or a "New-Lifer"?!	131
Purchased with the Blood of Christ!	133

Peter, feed my Lambs and Sheep!... 135
Prepare me a lodging!!.. 138
Remembering God's Chosen People!! 140
Stepping into the New Year with Jesus!...................................... 144
The Butterfly 146
The God who leads the Blind! 148
The Master has come 150
The Miracle of Easter! by George Jesze 151
The Missing Day or: Restoring the years!!.................................. 153
The Old Violin or: The Touch of the Master's Hand! 156
The Power of the Name!! 159
The Prayer of Jabez... 161
The Saga of the Toilet-Rolls!!... 164
There is Hope – for YOU!! 166
Trusting the Heavenly Father.. 169
Truth in the inward parts 171
Welcome, Holy Spirit! 173
Where shall I go? 176
Wills and Valentines! 178
The God who changes "It seems" by George Jesze................... 180
Worry or the Word?.. 183
Of Chickens and Sheep or: The God who Answers! 187
BIOGRAPHICAL DETAILS OF HELEN JESZE 190

Foreword

This book is compiled of the poems from my *Promise of Spring, Poems and Stories in Rhyme* book, and many newer poems, plus Inspirational Writings, including a few from my late husband, George.

In this world today, there are countless 'voices' shouting or speaking to us, and are clamouring for our attention. We get drawn here and there, trying to understand, take in all the information thrown at us, and often end up more confused than ever. However, there is ONE VOICE that constantly seeks to speak to us, which is not just noise; this is **God our Heavenly Father. His voice is vastly different! It comes not from his intellect, but from his HEART.**

He knows just where we are at the moment, either sailing merrily along as though everything in our particular garden is lovely, or whether we are broken and vulnerable, without hope because of what Life has brought our way, or as so many are today, fearful of what Tomorrow will bring.

In this book, I do not shy away from nitty-gritty, down-to-earth topics such as loneliness, death, sexual abuse, adultery, brokenness, world problems BUT bring answers from "the Father", His Son, our Lord Jesus Christ and the written Word of God. His unconditional love reaches out to you and me. His voice brings a message of love, hope, direction, peace after the storm. His message of protection and safety comes as he folds his wings about our life.

Thank you so much for taking time to read this book and it is my prayer that you will be greatly blessed and encouraged, and if you don't already know God as your "Father", that in these pages, you will find the way to do this!

Helen Jesze

Poems

"... **godliness with contentment is great gain.**" **1 Tim. 6:6**

Grandpa and Grandma

Grandma sat in the creaky chair in the corner by the fire there.
She sat in a rocker and rocked away, as she knitted kitty played
With the wool, a brightly-coloured ball. Trees outside stood tall
Guarding the old homestead. From the oven came the smell
                      of new bread.
Firelight shone on the old clock-face, tick-tock with its steady pace.
The brass warming-pan with leather bands, carefully polished
                      by loving hands;
At the window the curtain fluttered, on the hob a kettle sputtered.
Grandpa sat on the old oak settle --- a man of gentleness, of mettle.
A child sat on his substantial knee, a girl as mischievous as can be ---
I can't believe it ever was me!

                      ****

What I don't Understand

    What I don't understand I'll leave in his hand,
    He'll show me the way I should go.
    I'll not worry and fret and just try to forget
    About the things I should know.

    One day I shall see that he led me aright
    So I'll trust where I can't always trace.
    Then upon my path will continually shine
    The light from his wonderful face!

                      ****

Prodigal Sons and Daughters

Prodigal sons and daughters with feet that wander away
Trampling upon a moral code, God's laws and God's ways.
Wide eyes search for new things, look to horizons afar
Hands throw off what seem like chains, seek for a beckoning star.
Bodies that long for excitement -- the drug, the needle, the glue,
The booze, the weed, the pills, the rave, Ecstacy, snow, for you!
Stark heat and thrill of passion -- love, sex if they want every day.
Every dream you could ever dream. *My way*, they say, *my way!*

Pendulums, crystals and magic, Ouija-board, contact the dead
Lured by the unseen world of occult, caught in the spider's web.
Prodigal ears that are hearing the sound of the tempter's voice.
Prodigal eyes now seeing things which should not be their choice.
Turned from the God of their fathers, the wisdom sent from above
To a heart that this world has to offer, romance without true love.
Bubbles that burst at the touching, buds that could never flower.
Words that hold no substance which fail in the crucial hour.

Nothing to fill that deep longing, the emptiness deep down inside.
No light to pierce through the blackness, nowhere to run and hide.
No-one to lift the burden, no-one to set them free.
No-one to stop their headlong rush to Hell –- for eternity!
But God who is rich in mercy has followed them on their flight.
His voice is calling them in love from darkness back to light.
In the spirit-world he is busy although it's not yet seen.
He'll heal backslidings, freely love, as though it had never been.

Come to yourselves, sons and daughters, throw off the coils of sin.
Let the Word that's buried in your heart grow, come to life again.
Rise up from where you're sitting and make the decision to come
Back to the love that waits for you, back to the Father and Home!

****

Pick up the Tools

Pick up the tools that you laid down
And be encouraged, my friend.
Let your hands be strengthend today in God,
You'll be glad you believed till the victory came
When for you Life's journey will end.

Take up the song that you ceased to sing
When it seemed your heart was broken.
Let your voice ring out in a song of faith,
A new day for you is about to dawn,
For to you the promise is spoken!

Pick up the threads and let God weave
A beautiful pattern and plan,
When Life seemed bleak with your loved one gone,
Sunshine and colour will come once again.
When no-one can help you --- GOD CAN!

Pick up the Bible that you laid down
And read its message plain;
A message of comfort, of strength and hope,
A light and a guide for the days ahead
You'll find in its pages again!

****

"God saw all that he had made, and it was very good"
Gen. 1:31 NIV

Mists in the Morning

Mists in the morning, white clouds a-floating
And stars shining in the night.
Mists in the morning, white clouds a-floating
And stars shining ever so bright.

Red roses growing with poppies a-blowing

And song-birds singing their song.
Red roses growing and poppies a-blowing
And song-birds hop-hopping along.

Green leaves a-sprouting, horse-chestnut budding
And delicate spider-web.
Green leaves a-sprouting, horse-chestnut budding
And dew-spangled spider-web.

River a-flowing and thunder a-roaring
With ivy a-climbing the wall.
River a-flowing and thunder a-roaring
With ivy a-climbing so tall.

Bumble-bees buzzing with butterflies flitting
And bluebells that hide in the dell.
Bumble-bees buzzing and butterflies flitting
And bluebells and violets as well.

Red cows a-mooing with black lambs a-frisking
And mischievous children at play.
Red cows a-mooing with black lambs a-frisking
And children a-playing all day.

****

Joy comes in the Morning

Not a ray of light could I see on the horizon of my life.
Of course, there were some, but I was too benumbed
by pain, my eyes too clouded with tears, to see them.
What I said would never happen, had indeed happened.

It seemed there was no way out and grief would
drench me, crushing joy and life from me.
But as I stretched out my hands in silent, imploring
prayer, the words broke forth from deep within me:
My God, I thank you, sunshine and light will one day

rise upon the now-darkened horizon of my life.

And something rose within me, pushing its way thro'
the grief and self-pity; it was my "spirit-man", though
bruised and wounded, was drawing life from the stream
of God, like a pine-tree, temporarily weighed down by
snow, was springing back to its natural, upright position.

And the LIGHT came,
pale at first, struggling, often obscured by dark clouds of
doubt and discouragement, but *bursting forth* ---
in bright, shining, healing love!

How could it be otherwise?

**I HAD THE MENDER OF BROKEN HEARTS
LIVING WITHIN ME !!**

****

Harvest-Dream

Stark trees, bereft of leaves, standing high against the sky
Black-blue, skeletral, twig-fingers reach tall.
Delicate tracery, branches lacery. Soft touched, paint-brushed,
Burnished gold, now holds the morning sun who early come
From night sleep in rich deep thick loam soil, sees hard toil
Of strong man at the span. Here the force of the horse
Pulling now at the plough furrows straight towards a gate.
Rooks caw, sharp and raw, swallows wheel on the heel
Of curling whisps of ghostly mist. Clouds pink, rise, sink
Peep, tease between the trees. Rabbit tail white, runs in fright
On the run from farmer's gun. Plough turns as metal churns
Moist earth, prepare for birth of seed and wheat, enjoy and eat.

**Supervision of God's provision,
For a harvest golden we're beholden --
To the love of One above!**

****

Cry of India!

INDIA -- land of 'holy men', squalid huts and opium den.
Green rice-paddies, scorchèd earth, no harvest, famine, dearth.
Elephants huge, pushing logs near the mangy, stray street dogs.
Myriad children running wild, yet a person, each small child.
Sticklike legs and stooping back, buildings just about to crack.
Heaps of refuse in the street, honking horns and hurrying feet.
Rickshaws pulled by coolies thin. Cannot hear above the din.
Goats and pigs with traffic vie, endless people pushing by.
Holy cows have right of way through the city any day.
Urine-stench, sweet smell of drug, fly, mosquito, gnat and bug.
Pleading hands, beggar-blind, maimed, despicable, every kind.
None to hear their mournful cry, none to comfort when they die.
Lepers here, a frightful scene, a hole where once a nose has been.

Hindu-Temple, heathen shrine, demon-worship, priestly whine.
Burning bodies, wail for dead, anguished hearts and bowèd head.
Corpses lying on the stones, vultures feed upon their bones.
Disease and sickness, running sore, cup of misery flowing o'er!
Rushing flood or dried-up well, when we'll eat, we cannot tell!
Prostitutes and thieves abound, steal before you turn around!
Buses run-down, steaming trains, decaying houses, open drains.

Sitting down on the ground, charmer pipes to snake curled round.
Speakers blare music weird, dark brown faces with black beard.
Delicate sari, filthy rag, striking beauty, toothless hag.
Businessman in Western suit, bazaars of clothing, meat and fruit.
Hotel, office, building, school tell of long-gone British rule.

HAVE YOU HEARD MY MESSAGE HERE?
LET IT COME THROUGH LOUD AND CLEAR!
INDIA NEEDS YOUR HELP TODAY!
INDIA NEEDS THAT YOU SHOULD PRAY!

Take her needs upon your heart, make them of yourself a part.
Tell of One whose love brought Him down from Heaven above.
Ganges river will not bring forgiveness, cleansing, peace within.
And if you cannot GO, my friend,
YOU CAN GIVE, ANOTHER TO SEND.

The golden grain is ripening fast. Soon the harvest will be past.
India's night may soon come on, a chance to help may then be gone!
In the harvest you can share,

SHOW THEM THAT YOU REALLY CARE!!

****

Dawn-Chorus

I woke in the early morning, the day was cool and still,
But then I heard the song-thrush out on my window-sill.
With feathers sleek, breast puffed out he sang to welcome Day,
And in his song of joy and life the dark did melt away.
He sang for the joy of living the song of his Maker-Friend,
Whistled and chirped of a life beyond, a love that never ends.
His friend the sparrow on the branch of the horse-chestnut tree
Joined the song and sang along of a time that is yet to be.

They sang deep down into my heart; I listened enraptured there
At the beauty, energy, creative love of a feathered bird-song pair.
They did not ask for payment or if anyone had heard,
Just followed the urge the Maker-Friend placed within each bird.
Liquid notes of beauty which soothe an anguished heart,
Pouring like oil over gaping wounds, touching an inward part
Of the man who wrapped in sorrow can't bear to face the day,
Telling of One who heals broken hearts, in the desert makes a way.

Their song called forth in me new praise to this great Maker-Friend
For the peace and joy that he gives, and a love which will never end.
For the gift of sight and the gift of song that I am able to hear,
So I'll listen to the message that they bring to me ---
These birds in the garden near.

****

Silent Scream

"O let me live!" a silent scream from lips as yet unformed.
A "creature", "clump of cells", but no, a *child* that's yet unborn.

Fruit of love or fruit of lust within a woman's guarding womb.
Now the woman wonders: Should my womb become a tomb?

Searching knife, cutting blade, machine that sucks and rips apart
Or salt solution that will burn, destroy this baby's bleeding heart.

Cause the love of Motherhood, great God of Mercy now we pray,
To speedily spring forth that she, with all her heart would say

I've heard your cry, my little one, despite what everyone might say
My love gives you the right to live, ***for you it is not night but day!***

****

Abused Restored!!

"Don't let him come tonight!" she pleads
Then pulls the covers up so high
As if that they could keep at bay
Those groping hands and heavy thighs,

The sheer brute force and searing pain,
Dark eyes of lust and tortured face
Inflicting power, laughs at control
Over the prey, no mercy-grace.

Curled in fetal position she
As unborn child within the womb
Yet without safety she's exposed
Her heart a catastrophic tomb
Of broken hopes and long-dead dreams
Innocence robbed, a crushed, weak flower
Emotions locked in an iron cage
Walled up in an impervious tower.

But One has seen that breaking heart
Has heard the silent scream within,
His love an ointment on the wounds
His cleansing blood for every sin.
That presence like a blanket warm
Wraps round her in her cold, dark night
Brings spark of hope which later turns
Into assurance, blinding light.

God of compassion, in his Son
Who came to seek and save the lost
And mend the struggling, bleeding ones
Redeem them at tremendous cost.
Come now and with your gentle hand
Lift up this bruised and frightened child.
Open the cage, break down the tower
Bring joy and healing with your smile.

**Let all Life's broken pieces here
In your hand take mosaic form
That all may see what you can do
Such strength and beauty, colours warm.
Lord Jesus Christ, Anointed One
We know you will not pass her by
But you will cause her now to walk**

Whole and restored, with head held high!

****

After YOU, Lord, will I run!!

"Draw me, we will run after thee ..." Song of Solomon 1:4a

I'll doubt my doubts and my fears, trust in Him who thro' the years
Has guided me and He should know, surely the way that I must go.
His gracious face it smiles on me, He calls and my reply will be:
You have drawn me, I will come, *After you, Lord, will I run!*

Lovely Jesus, Pearl divine, greater than all treasures mine –
Rarer than the lily fair blooming in the garden there.
Wondrous, shining, Morning Star, Light upon my path you are.
Comfort of my lonely hour, turns my thorn into a flower.

Takes me through the waters deep, keeps my often faltering feet
Causes them to jump and run, makes my path a plain straight one.
Brings me thro' the furnace heat, in earth's sorrow gives comfort sweet,
Unsinged, unharmed, no fiery smell, for Jesus doeth all things well!

Makes my desert bud and flower. His Name is like a mighty tower,
All are safe who run within, safe from danger, fear and sin.
Lovely Jesus, Pearl divine, greater than all treasures mine.
You have called me, I will come – *After you, Lord, will I run!*

****

A Trysting-Place

I knew he was coming. I felt him draw near.
His presence and glory preceded his 'tangible' form.
Not seeing, not knowing why, how and wherefore
Yet *knowing* that *he* was coming to meet *me*.
A trysting-place one would have called it years ago,
Where two lovers come to meet and show their love;

Where words are spoken fit only for the other's ears
And hidden away in the heart;
Secrets, intimacies are shared, understood only by these two,
My Heavenly Bridegroom and I.

Longing to hold him, I stretch out my physical arms to embrace,
And *know* he wraps his spiritual arms around me.
He is real, as real as the air I breathe.
His presence envelops me. Thrills my inner being with rapture,
Comfort, assurance and security wash around and through me,
Lulling me to peace, in the midst of the storm.
No-one like you, Jesus Christ, Lord of my life!
No-one like you! He whispers in return.
No-one like you, child of my heart!

As I lay against this heart, I catch the beat, the throb
Urgent, strong, with longing, intensity and agony
The throb of Love unrequited, unreturned, spurned

Rejected by millions of his own creatures.
Yet this love still streams out. It cannot stop,
For then *he* would cease to *exist*, for *he is Love.*
This is the *risk* of Love, the risk that the loved one
Will not return love, but will laugh and scorn
Such a marvellous treasure.

But you went further than this risk, Lord Jesus,
You stepped right over it, ignoring its doubts and its fears,
Ran to meet me with outstretched arms, welcoming,
Inviting me to have fellowship – to become yours alone!
Take this Calvary-Love! Let it flow from my heart into yours.
Now you be a carrier, a bearer of this love to all those
Who have not yet experienced it, I hear you command,
For I came to heal the broken hearts in this world.

****

A Garment of Praise

There is a garment so sweet to wear,
A garment of praise, of song and prayer;
Prepared for his own redeemed, loved band,
Especially woven by the Master's hand.
A garment so cool for the hottest day
When peril or temptation comes in our way,
But warm as a coat in the Winter's snow
When the winds of disappointment blow.
And though it's so light, it's strong as steel,
That through it the wearer cannot feel
The fiery darts which at him fly
When the enemy of souls is masquerading by.
Prepared for his own redeemed, loved band,
Especially woven by the Master's hand.
The worldly fashions come and go
But this one will never outdate, I know.
It's as new and as good when worn today,
As the garment of praise worn yesterday.
And even tomorrow so it will be,
As it's fashioned for Eternity.
Come, friend, are you feeling the cold?
Has your garment of praise become torn and old?
It can be renewed very quickly, you know,
If straight to the Saviour you will go.
Remember God's love and what he has done,
And how in his mercy sent Jesus his Son
That instead of dark, lonely and sin-governed days,
You might wear for him -----
A garment of praise!

****

Bird-Song

He sang for me in the morning after a long, dark night.
He sang for me at noon-day when the sun was at its height.

But his song was stilled as shadows descended on the lane
Yet I know that soon my little friend will sing for me again.

He comforted me in the morning after a long, dark night.
He rejoiced with me at noonday, when the sun was at its height.
But his voice was stilled as shadows descended upon Life's lane
Yet I know that soon, Jesus my Friend, will speak to me again!

****

Cast your Care upon Him

Cast your care upon him for he careth for you
The words on my heart fell as cool as the dew,
For I'd thought that no love could be ever so true,
Cast your care upon him for he careth for you.

Cast your care upon him for he careth for you
Let sorrow's deep wound feel the comfort anew.
He said, Do not fear, my strong arms are round you
Cast your care upon him for he careth for you!

Cast your care upon him for he careth for you
Behind those dark clouds there's a Heaven so blue.
O my soul, then recall till the sun's shining through
Cast your care upon him for he careth for you!

****

Church on the Hill

Church on the hill, spire pierces the sky, slate-grey roof.
Walls white, oak door, iron-studded, creaks at your push.
A small chapel interior, step inside, sit on a notched pew.
Carpet once red, but worn now with several generations
Of religious, bored or seeking feet.
A small but adequate altar, gold-fringed cloth, two white

Candles burning, non-dripping and steady.
The massive Bible lies open on the lecturn.
Stained-glass windows with shafts of red, blue, yellow light.
Pull out the hassock, embroidered tapestry --
Kneel and pray. "God, where are you?"
A voice in your heart replies: "I'm here, I will not leave you."
Rise up comforted, out through the old, oak door,
Creaking at your push, down the hill ...
Going --- with his peace.

****

The House on the Hill

The house on the hill has a red roof and a fir-tree pointing high.
Deer run wild in the woods behind and a blue, clear Summer sky.
It seems to me like yesterday we trod the path that wound
Thro' purple heather and yellow gorse, with Jip bounding around.

Then as we entered the old, oak door we saw the winding stair
Every nook and corner we loved and Dad's old favourite chair.
A bowl of daffodils, yellow and bright proclaimed Spring
                                        had been here;
Aunt Mary's text hung on the wall: It is I --- be of good cheer!

I've travelled o'er the sea, been far and wide; I've said it and say it
                                                                                                   still:
You'll never find a place like this dear old home ---
                                        The red-roofed house on the hill!

****

Come away, my Love

Come away, my love, come away with me, the dove's sweet voice is heard.
Flowers spring up and appear in the land, on every bough there sings a bird.
    Shake off your heavy Winter shoes, put on the Gospel of peace.
   Come, dance in praise for my delight, my love for you will never cease.

     How beautiful you are to me. I have washed you white as snow.
   Although you had many lovers before, from me you will never go.
Calling your name from the mountains high, searching thru' valleys low
  Finding you, I carried you home with me, from me you will never go.

The Winter was long and very cold, the trees were shrivelled and bare.
No life, no green in the world to be seen, Winter reigned everywhere.
I have risen as the Sun of righteousness, the ice and the snow did thaw,
  My rainbow arches over the earth — sign of mercy as never before.

    Your ear was slow to hear the voice of the turtle-dove so sweet.
   I sent Him out to call for you, but you ran away on nimble feet.
      Until at last I won your love, then he led you to my side.
I am your Saviour, Lover and Lord, you are my chosen, holy bride.

  Sit in my shadow, I will shelter you from the heat of a noonday sun.
Come to my heart, let me hold you there, I want that you and I be one.
    Put on a dress of purest white, you will shine and gleam from afar
       Like a city set upon a hill. They call me the Morning Star.

   You will never fail, you will never fall if you look into my face.
    As we walk along the road of Life just trust my wondrous grace.
     And if at times you don't see me there, I'm really very near.
Round Faith's corner I'll suddenly come, with joy my voice you'll hear.

I can hear your song of love to me, my heart is satisfied.
This moment with joy I did anticipate, yes, even before I died.
To purchase my bride I went alone up Calvary's hill one day,
But my Father brought me back to life; together we'll live always.

Come away, my love, come away with me,
Let me take you by the hand.
Come away, my love, come away with me,
Come into Resurrection-Land!

****

Come my Daughter – give me the Key!

**"He heals the brokenhearted and binds up their wounds,"
Ps. 147:3 NIV**

**Holy Spirit, you show me there are doors within me,
Doors I have shut tight
Locking them and hiding the key
That I might not need to look behind them.
The memories, bitter griefs, hurtful situations
I have stored in there.**

**Yet time and again, in self-torture and self-pity
I have entered these rooms of my mind
And wandered among those negative things of the Past.
I have stopped here and there, examining, re-living,
Hearing the angry or despairing words
Amazingly, startlingly clear
Although spoken long ago.**

**As the hurt swelled and magnified,
Threatening to swamp me,
In panic I ran out, banging the doors.
I locked them tightly, hid the key
And made the decision to never look again.**

But now you are knocking on those doors, Holy Spirit,
Gently, insistently, saying: *Let me in!*
I will cleanse and heal every wound
You still carry deep within your heart.
Every room of your life shall be filled
With the sunshine and presence,
The glory of the Lord!

This is the way to be truly whole.
Come, my daughter, *give me the key!*

****

Country-Treasures

Away from the noise and the rush of the city
Away from the bustle and pushing around.
Out to the fields and sights of the country
Early when morning-dew's fresh on the ground.

Away from the buildings and bridges and traffic
Office-blocks high --- just concrete and glass.
Under the dome of God's blue Heaven
Walking with pleasure on springy, green grass.

Away from the time-table, schedule, appointment
Looking at watches and missing the train.
Remembering that Time is a speck in Eternity
Learning to relax and breathe free again.

Away from the darkness and gloom of old alleys
Broken-down passages of brick and stone.
Out in the brilliance and warmth of the sunshine,
Shake off despondency, feeling alone.

Walk through the village and down the green valley
Climb to a summit, lie under a tree.
Listen to bird-song, the rush of the river --
These are the treasures just waiting for me!

****

Don't scratch with the Chickens

Don't scratch with the chickens there in the dust
But fly with the eagle on high!
Don't grovel and crawl and fight and fuss
But set your goal to the sky.

Up like the eagle, towards the sun
Building your home high not low.
Wary and watching for serpents who'd come
Watching your little ones grow.

Up, far above where the other birds sit
There on the telephone wire,
Chatt'ring their gossip, every tit-bit,
Fly eagle, fly really higher!

The chickens they scratch in dirt for their food
Always they look at the ground.
Why not eat something that's fresh and good,
God's Word is very good, I have found.

Teaching the new, little eagles to fly,
Bearing them up on his wings.
Father supports us when trouble is nigh,
Making us conquering kings!

****

For such a Time!

Born for such a time, for such a time as this, born for this generation.
Born for this time in the Father's plan to meet the needs of the nations.
Prepared in secret, refined in the fire, strong to face temptation

Grounded in the Word, walking in the light, humble, no condemnation.

Born for such an hour, for such an hour as this, the hour of this generation.
Born for this hour in the Father's plan to meet the needs of the nations.
People of vision inspired by God, not moved by earthly sensation.
Consumed by love, our finger on the pulse of a dying, deceived generation.

Born for such a task, for such a task as this, born for this generation.
Born for this task in the Father's plan to meet the needs of the nations.
Our ears and spirits tuned ready to hear his divine instruction.
Those strategies he shows for saving the lost from eternal destruction.

Born to give birth, even spiritual birth, born for this generation
Born to bring forth in the Father's plan to meet the needs of the nations.
A tool that's fashioned for a purpose sure, an arrow shot from his bow
Ablaze with the fire of the Holy Spirit, our lips and hearts aglow!

Born for such a time, for such a time as this, born for this generation.
Born for this time in the Father's plan to meet the needs of the nations!

****

For Love of Mary --- Meditation on Luke 7:36-50

Creeping around the marble pillars, holding her skirts lest they brush the velvet curtains, round the tables, until she stands behind the Master. Raven hair escaping from her veil, something clutched in her hand. The sunlight catches tear-drops which are trickling slowly and with increasing intensity, down olive cheeks. Even through her wide Eastern dress, it is easy to see her beauty and grace, easy to understand why many a man could not say No. She was only too willing, looking for Love and to be wanted.

What does she want here? Here in Simon's house, at the dinner he has given for the Master and his followers. Does she think she

can seduce Him too --- this strange miracle-worker from Galilee?!
Women *have* followed Him, left home to hear His words, see His
miracles. Joanna, the wife of Chuza, Herod's steward, Susanna
and others who supported His cause. But never in *that* way.

Why, she's kneeling down behind Him and has taken off her veil!
No bold, coquettish manner now. She looks broken, bowed as if
years of intense longing and grief pour out of her being, at the
Master's feet. Why look, His feet are very dirty. Didn't Simon give
water to wash them? Eastern hospitality would make it impossible
to forget that! Tears are making rivulets in the grey dust on His feet,
now ever widening and widening until the dust is washed away …

Watching, half-turned, as He reclines on His couch at the table, the
Master's eyes are deeply tender. A ripple goes through the crowd. If
this Man were a prophet, He would know it's a slut touching Him!
This accusation has hardly filled Simon's heart when, penetratingly,
Jesus looks and says: "Simon, I have something to say to you.
Flushed with wine and pride, Simon graciously nods him to proceed.

"A man loaned money, $5000 to one, $500 to the other. Neither could
pay him back, so he kindly forgave both and let them keep the money."
Simon's attention is diverted from the Master's story to this woman,
who is now --- of all things --- wiping the tear-washed feet with her
hair and breaking a flask of expensive ointment over them.
The eyes of all the guests are upon this tableau, only Mary is
unconscious of their stares. She is lost in worship, grief, joy
grief for past sins, but joy because here is One

WHO IS THE EMBODIMENT OF TRUE LOVE.

The Master's voice comes clear, penetrating, pointedly now:
"Simon, which of these men will love their creditor the most?"
Wondering what Jesus is getting at, Simon replies: "I think, he
who was forgiven the most." Jesus says: "See this woman ---
As I entered the house, you gave me no water for my feet; she
has washed them WITH HER TEARS, WIPED THEM WITH
HER HAIR. You gave me no kiss of greeting, but this woman,
since I came in, HAS NOT CEASED TO KISS MY FEET."

Beads of perspiration roll down Simon's fat, sly face. The dinner
to impress his friends and Jesus has not turned out as planned.
But there is no escape, for the accusing voice goes on: "My head

you did not anoint, but she has ANOINTED MY FEET WITH OINTMENT. So, I say, her sins which are many are forgiven, for she loved much; but to whom little is forgiven, like you, morally upright Simon, but with a cold heart, the same LOVES LITTLE."

Turning to the woman and lifting her gently from the floor, he says:

"Woman, your sins are forgiven!"

A marvellous smile of joy and wonder breaks over her face and she turns, goes round the tables, past velvet curtains and marble pillars, raven hair escaping from her veil, but with nothing in her hand ---

The empty ointment-flask is where it had rolled --- in the corner.

****

It's the Christ of the Cross

It's the Christ of the cross not the cross of the Christ
That's redeemed me and saved my soul.
It's the stripes on his back from the cruel Roman lash
That from sickness have made me whole.
Not a cross on a chain that's hung round my neck
Is a guarantee from evil and fear
But the blood of Jesus Christ that was shed on Calvary
Brings deliverance and protection to me here!

****

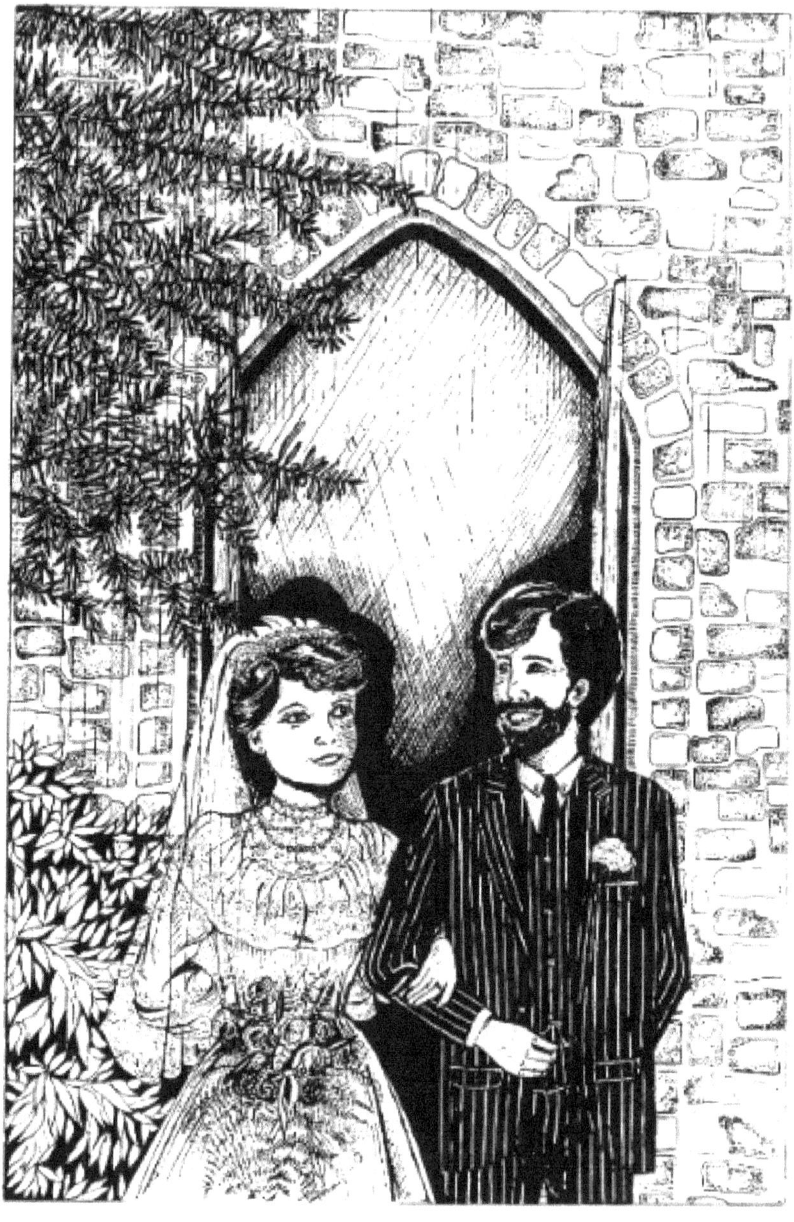

To the Bride and Groom

Bride and groom, there they stand, wife and husband hand in hand.
Going forward from this day on a new untrodden way.
What lies before they do not know, but confident with joy they go
Knowing that their Lord above will keep them in his perfect love.
A happy home is always sure when faith is strong and love is pure.
We would tell you: Guard your heart so you might not drift apart
In the pressures felt in Life, bringing with them care and strife.
Learn to love each other more than you've ever done before,
And forgive if things go wrong, let your wrath be short not long
Don't just take, learn to give. This is the rule if happy you'd live!

God made you different than your mate, and so accept his plan.
One is quiet, the other is loud; one likes peace, the other a crowd.
And so let each completed be in each other's personality.
Let the Bible be your guide as you're walking side by side,
And the Holy Spirit lead, then you'll have all that you need.
There in Eden, Adam and Eve first found Love, I do believe.
Many misuse it I've heard tell, so take this gift and use it well!
Now --- MR and MRS, BRIDE and GROOM
We wish you a happy honeymoon!!

****

Greater than All

Greater than all the mistakes I have made, Greater than every wrong done
Greater than every wrong word I've said. Greater than wrong songs I've sung.

Greater than times when I've gone my own way, Greater than hate 'stead of love
Greater than fog which shrouds all my day, Greater than dark skies above.

Greater than doubts assailing my mind, Greater than wrong paths I've trod.
Greater than negative thoughts of all kinds, Greater than all things,
Greater than all things, Greater than all things –

This is my, this is my GOD!

****

Heather Country

The bird-house hangs in the apple-tree
                    by the house down near the heather
Now dead-brown from Winter-time
                    yet in glorious Summer weather
Becomes a riot of lilac and purple brush, bells pink and white
Edged by miles of dark trees tall, moor – without end in sight.

The bird-house holds some secrets proud, a nest is neatly made
And a mother-bird in this early Spring her eggs has already laid.
I watch her from my bedroom window fluttering on the tree
Her mate cocks his head, answering her excitement that's
                                      plain to see.

Waiting for a dress of fresh, green leaves,
                    branches point down to the grass
Out to the sides and up to the eaves, take no notice as we pass
The old apple-tree, mossed and lichened so near I could
                                  touch its fingers
But I'll not disturb for a blue-tit rests, a blackbird also lingers.

I've made up my mind to come again to stay
                            in the house by the heather
To enjoy the miracle of Nature's bursting forth in Summer weather.
The bird-house will be empty then, its babies have come and gone.
They'll be flying through God's blue, blue sky
                                for that's how Life goes on!

****

He came to me

He came to me when the night was long; it seemed to never end.
He came to me when black despair upon my heart did descend.
He came and with his loving care relieved, delivered me,
Brought light at which darkness fled, he calmed my troubled sea.

He came and took the hand that clutched at the silent, empty air.
He came to breathe his pulsing life in my spirit bowed with care.
He came the silver tears to catch in the bottle that he kept
As with contrite heart, in brokenness, I before him wept.

He came to whisper a song of praise when heaviness weighted me.
He caused me to smile and laugh again, gone was my agony.
He came as the storm beat on my boat, commanded: Peace, be still!
He came and you know he's never left --- **and I know he never will!**

****

Holy Spirit, I'm hungry for you!

Holy Spirit, I'm hungry for you!
And not just for what you can do.
O, I ask in Jesus' Name
Set my heart aflame!
Holy Spirit, I'm hungry for you!

Holy Spirit, I'm thirsty for you!
Let your living water wash me right thru'.
O, burn with holy fire
Every sinful desire!
Holy Spirit, I'm thirsty for you!

Holy Spirit, I'm searching for you.
You're the Spirit of Wisdom and Truth.

Fill me now with love and power
For this dynamic hour!
Holy Spirit, I'm searching for you!

Holy Spirit, I cry now to you!
O, I want to discover you anew!
Be creative in me
That the world now may see
The wonders of what you can do!

George and Helen

****

I refuse to worry

I refuse to worry, I refuse to fret
For my God is on the throne, he's never failed me yet!
I'll cast my care upon him and let him care for me,
For the Greater One in me gives me the victory!

I refuse to question and ask why things turned out
Different than I thought that they would surely come about.
And over every onslaught of the enemy I know
God will bring me through unscathed, his Word says it is so!

Shake the chains from off your neck, O People of the Lord
Faith must laugh at circumstances and believe the Word.
Disregard the symptoms, by his stripes you are healed!
One day soon, you'll see the glory of the Lord revealed!

Victory in the morning when the day is not so bright.
Victory in the midst of fear in your darkest night.
Victory when the storms of doubt buffet and assail,
He, who does the Word of God, his faith will prevail!

****

I'll be with you

I'll be with you in the morning and with you through the day
I'll be with you when evening shadows fall across your way.
I'll be with you in good times and when storms toss you around,
With my Peace, be still! to calm the waves, put your feet on solid ground.

I'll be with you at every crossroad telling you which way to go
If decisions press and questions come, and you don't know Yes or No.
I'll impart to you my wisdom, with my Spirit I will lead
To waters still and pastures green, where you in peace will feed.

I'll be with you when you're grieving about mistakes made in the past
If regrets and torment fill your mind --- the Devil says, I've got you fast!
Don't listen to his lying words, but take the Word I've said
From mistakes and sin I've washed you clean in the precious blood I shed!

I'll be with you till that morning, I'll be with you till that day
When you stand before Heaven's door at the end of your earthly way.
I'll be with you till we greet each other joyfully face to face,
When I hold you child, to my breast, and you'll see it was all my grace!

****

I'm in his Hand

I'm in his hand, I'm in his hand, I will not fear, I'm in his hand.
And tho' I cannot always understand, I'm in his nail-scarred hand.

I'm near his side, I'm near his side, and evermore I'll here abide.
From the storm he will me always hide, I'm near his spear-thrust side.

I'm under his wings, I'm under his wings, they cover me from everything.
Tho' the world round me rock and swing, I'm under his overshadowing wings.

I'm at his feet, I'm at his feet, and there we'll have fellowship sweet.
And Oh, this makes my happiness complete, I'm at his nail-piercèd feet.

****

In Quietness and in Confidence

I sighed for the moon when I had the Sun which had risen in my heart.
I longed for the stars tho' I had the Chief who would never more depart.
I cried for a trumpet-voice to command when deep within my soul
The words were written with piercèd hand: Be thou under my control!
I gazed to horizons cloudy, dim, with between Time's gulf so planned
But I could not see the pleas for help already placed at my hand.
I sought for Gilead's pleasant balm my broken heart to heal
But was not able his precious calm through pain and unrest to feel.
How could I lift this heavy cross, much less bear it to the end?
But I did not know *his* was the loss, *he* 'neath its weight did bend.
I ran for a weapon with which to charge in the battle raging there.
But if I'd seen, no need would have been, I had the weapon of prayer.
I looked again and seeing then a figure upon its knees,
My Saviour, sweating drops of blood under Gethsemane's trees.
Then as he drank the bitter cup down to the dregs of sin and loss
Foresaw all the pain and shame which waited for him at the cross ---
It seemed I caught a sudden glimpse of what he'd done for me,
Doing the Will of the Father and going to Calvary.
Unrest and hurry seeped away for then I saw at length
In quietness and confidence --- yes, that would be my strength.
Laying still in the Saviour's hand, knowing God's Will is best,
Letting him have his perfect way --- *entering into his rest!*

****

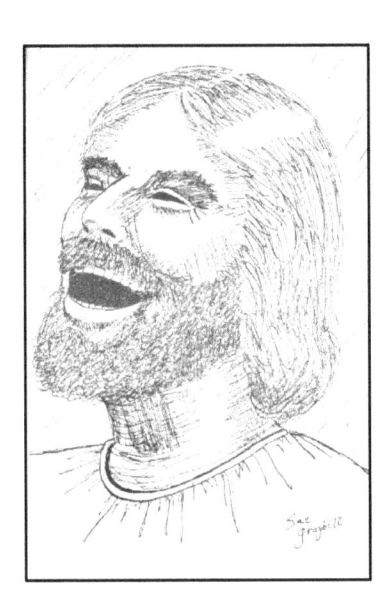

"... having spoiled principalities and powers, he made a shew of them openly, triumphing over them in it ." Colossians 2:15 KJV

Laughing Jesus

I saw a picture yesterday of Jesus Christ with laughing face ---
A face just full of sheer delight, of radiance after a long night
And beaming grace.

And as I looked yet again, it seemed he laughed at some big joke.
It seemed to bubble from within, like a hidden, refreshing spring;
Of joy it spoke.

I think he must have laughed at how he had nailed Satan to the wall
Put him to an open shame! Then God gave Jesus His great Name ---
High above all!

****

Just the Next Step

Just the next step that he wants me to take Only one step at a time.
Not lagging back or running ahead, Keeping in step with my Saviour divine.

Just the next thing that he wants me to do, knowing he'll guide me aright
Not wasting strength thro' impatience or fear, He makes me conqueror in every fight!

****

Let my Heart be in your Hand

Let my heart be in your hand that you might turn it
Like the streams of water wheresoe'er you will.
For you understand my thoughts, motives and desires
And you alone my longings can fulfill.
Let my heart be in your hand and mould it Jesus
To the fashion and the plan you've made for me.
Let its clamourings be silent as my ear is tuned to hear
Your voice that speaks so clear, so lovingly …

So I'll give you all my dreams and all my desires
And I'll give you all the wishes and all the fires
That burn within my heart, I would ask you, Lord,
To purify them with your Word.

I will quieten my heart before you my Saviour.
I will quieten my heart before you my Lord.
For it is my desire to receive your favour
For it is my desire to receive your Word.
I will say to my heart with all of its longings
Be still, let the Spirit of God work in you.
In the sunshine and shadows
Of Life's daily throngings

Let the hand of the Lord now come upon you!

****

Live in the Now!

I do not need to know the future that lies before me or details far ahead
Just to know the next step to take, the next thing that waits to be done.
Unborn years beckoning in the distance are not mine to approach today.
I was created to live in the NOW, not in the future or yesterday.

The knowledge of what tomorrow holds would be a burden;
If thro' impatience or curiosity I seek to discover it, I shall be marred.
As sand falls a grain at a time in the glass, so will I live my life
With its millions of seconds in a year –- steadily …. one at a time.

As the car headlights beam on the road showing the next few feet,
So will the lamp of his Word light my path, cheering, directing, guiding, warning of danger.

Leaving earthly ambition, I take *his* will and plan,
I will pray, work, hold that nail-scarred hand,
Trusting, as he lives his life –- through me.

Helen and George Jesze

****

Never be a Time!

Never be a time I'll not need Jesus, never be a time I'll not need him.
There will never be a moment I can manage Life on my own
In the heat of battle, he helps me to win.

There'll never be a day I'm self-sufficient
Enough to find the answer to every need.
When Life's shadows creep so far that Time has ceased to be
Then I'll see that One on whom I have believed.

****

Out of my Way!

The things you worry about at present, are so small, insignificant.
Although I know they seem large to you.
They fill your horizon, cause you to stumble, block your path.
Your heart threatens to burst with the pain, your mind is a-whirl
with questions of how such a thing could be or happen.

But seen with *my* eyes, through the eye of *Faith*
In the clarity and perspective which my Word gives
You will see your concerns shrink, become of minor importance.

**Something to laugh at --- to point your finger at
Saying boldly: In the Name of Jesus,
Out of my way!
Grace, grace to this mountain,
And they must obey!**

****

But just a Stepping-Stone

Although the way but darkness seems to me, still he leads on.
Never in the midst of sorrow leaves me there, the battle not yet won.
But on before, his footsteps glist'ning bright with blood upon this thorny way,
Still stepping onward, he my light, to lead me into everlasting day.
With blood?
Yes, for did he not to Calvary tread, the darkest path, the shadow of a cross,

Death's fear of pain and dread, all 'cept his Father's Will but loss?
How can *I* then but follow still with Calvary's scenes fresh in my soul
And yield to your almighty Will, till it becomes of me –- the whole!
Till I lay down earthly desire, those loves, those hopes which me from you would take.
Burn out the dross with your most holy fire and from a broken pile a better vessel make.

Help me to see your hand of love allows happiness and weary hours;
If I would grow more like unto yourself above, there surely will be sunshine and the showers.
But you are there, close by my side, and yet behind, and yet before,
For in *yourself* I'm hidden safe until this fearful storm be o'er.
Now through the gloom with glad anticipation I see my resurrection-morn appear.
It's darkest hour before Faith's realisation –- Keep on, he says, there's nought to fear.
Those things in darkness stumbled o'er when with tear-dimmed eyes you felt alone,
Seen with *Faith's* eyes, the darkness will be cleared
And they'll become but JUST A STEPPING-STONE!

****

Let my People go!

O Land of the North, let my people go forth,
    you've kept them imprisoned far too long.
I've heard their sad cry, and I'll not pass them by,
    but show them my arm is still strong.
In the camps and ghettos I've walked by their side,
    and so few have recognised me.
Weary and faint they've forgotten their God,
    but one day I'll set them all free.
Already I've planted a seed in their hearts,
    a longing for true liberty.
It's growing and stretching, yes, it will bring forth,
    and it's passion the whole world will see.

Oppressed and afflicted they'll not be denied
    though 'Pharaoh' has hardened his heart.
The day will come when this proud land too,
    must say, "My God, how great thou art!"
A veil has been over their eyes for a while,
    they've not seen that Messiah has come.
But the God of Abraham, Isaac and Jacob

>   will show them Jeshua is his Son!
> I've been telling my people there in the West
>   that Exodus II will take place,
> And they are preparing sweet havens of rest
>   to show them my love and my grace.
>
> With precision I am moving according to plan
>   and putting in place every piece.
> Jehovah will not be thwarted by man.
>   *Obey!* Or I'll give you no peace!
> So --- land of the North, let my people go forth,
>   let your borders and gates open wide.
> Let the young and the old, the sick and the sad
>   walk out into freedom at my side!

****

See them Coming

See them coming, from the Land of the North they've come.
When iron gates the prey will yield, I will be their sun and shield
To bring them safely home.
Now see them stream, from the Land of the North they'll stream.
A mighty flood of refugees --- old, young, the weak, diseased,
Say not, 'tis but a dream!

Now take them in, from the Land of the North they've come!
Put out the Welcome lamp at night, weary travellers love a light
And open to them your home.
Sit them down, sit them down, they have travelled far and long.
Faces etched by suffering's pen will light with joy and gladness
When I bring my people home.

You have the chance, you have the chance
To help my people on their way.
To give them food and clothes and love
In the Name of Jeshua from above ---
Prepare your heart today!

****

Return of the Exile

When the Lord turned again the captivity of Zion
We were like unto them that dream.
When the Lord turned again the captivity of Zion
How wonderful it did seem.
Our mouth was filled with laughter and our tongue with singing,
They said among the heathen, The Lord has done a great thing!
The Lord has done great things for us, whereof we are glad.
The Lord has done great things for us, we need no longer be sad!

We took our harps from the willows by the river, from the
                                         willows hanging green and low.
We took our harps from the willows by the river, singing
                                         up and down we did go.
We played the beloved songs of Judah and the songs of Israel,
Songs of the God of Heaven and Earth, who has done all things well!
The Lord has done great things for us whereof we are glad.
The Lord has done great things for us, we need no longer be sad!

****

Resting in the Lord

Come now, tired lamb, lie on my breast, nestle in my arms, learn to rest.
You've gone through the briars, you've gone through the fires.
The path has been rough, the way has been tough.
Come now, tired lamb, lie on my breast, nestle in my arms, learn to rest.

****

Rainbow Talk

Consider the rainbow I set in the sky
That speaks of my mercy and grace
When condemnation would paralyse you
So much that you can't see my face.
It's colours shine brightly after storm,
After rain, so let it speak always to you
My blood will suffice for every sin,
Above all things, your God is true!

My Lord loves me, and oh, the wonder I see
A rainbow shines in my window, the Lord loves me.
My Lord saved me on the cross of Calvary
He walks beside me each day to Eternity.

Not at the rainbow's end, not in a fairy-tale
I've found my crock of gold.
Gold that will never melt nor ever fade
Gold in Jesus Christ my Lord.
No-one can rob me of this treasure divine
No-one can tell me that it is not mine.
Wonderful assurance fills my heart today
My greatest treasure is found in his way.

Sweeter than honey, sweeter than honey his love to me
Precious, precious, more precious than gold
Is the love of my Saviour, more than I'd ever been told.
Beautiful, beautiful, so beautiful his face
Altogether lovely One, glorious his grace!

****

Roll, roll the Stone away

Roll, roll the stone away and let the risen Christ come forth.
Roll, roll the stone away and then his beauty you'll behold.
Roll away the doubt and fear, he the Prince of Peace
Wants to bring you to that place where all struggles cease.

Roll away the worry and care, for he said he'll care for you.
Cast your problems on the Lord, he will surely see you thro'.
He, the resurrected Christ who conquered in that hour
Wants to spring forth in your life by his mighty power.

Wipe, wipe away your tears, this is not the time to cry.
God is working in your life, you will see it bye and bye.
Nothing is impossible for Jesus Christ the Lord
When you lean your weight on him, trusting in his Word.

****

Sometimes it seems

Sometimes it seems that Satan is grinning,
sometimes it seems he's having his way.
Sometimes it seems wickedness is winning,
sometimes it seems that he's won the day.
Sometimes it seems God's losing the fight,
sometimes it seems evil triumphs over right.
Sometimes it seems the devil's on the throne,
sometimes it seems God's forsaken his own.
Sometimes it seems that the battle is lost,
sometimes it seems at a terrible cost.
Sometimes it seems that God's given in,
sometimes it seems that we'll never win.
Sometimes it seems all effort's in vain,
sometimes you feel there's no end to the pain.
Sometimes it seems Satan's stolen the show,
sometimes it seems the saints just don't know.
Sometimes it seems your day will not dawn,
sometimes it seems after night is no morn.
Sometimes it seems God's somewhere up there
sometimes it seems he just doesn't care.
Sometimes it seems the Winter is long,
sometimes it seems birds have all lost their song.
Sometimes it seems there's no Spring in the air,

just dark discouragement and despair.
Sometimes it seems that the saints are so small,
sometimes it seems that wrong's standing tall.
Sometimes it seems Satan's smarter than God,
for we've forgotten the power of the blood.

Sometimes --- but only sometimes is the case,
one wonderful day our struggles will cease.
The tide will turn, all battles will be won,
the sun will shine when that final day comes!
Satan's been defeated we read in the Word,
all power's been given to Jesus our Lord.
'Sometimes it seems' will vanish like a fog,
all powers must bow before Almighty God!

George and Helen Jesze

****

That first Easter

O to see the thorn-crowned head, reed-sceptred hand and purple dress
Of Jesus in the judgement-hall, as Pilate cried: Behold the Man!
And washed his beggar-noble hands, a King stood there before them all.
How little did they know that he who soon to Calvary would go
Beneath the heavy blood-stained cross was Son of God in flesh below.
Let me see the ruined hands which once on shining heads were pressed
Naked, speared by Roman hand, where John had laid his head, his breast.
O that my eyes were filled with tears a little more like those he shed
As near the olive-trees he lay, then as he drank the cup he bled.

O precious cup, then filled with myrrh and bitterest aloes for your soul
Filled with blessing, peace and love for me, a sinner you've made whole!
Then in the tomb I see him there, so cold in Death his form does lie;
But now I see him too, in Hell, and from proud Satan wrench the key
For he --- my Jesus --- could not long die!
Like Mary in the chill of morn, I too, with her would softly run
And carry spice and balm so sweet for the body of God's precious Son.
O wondrous truth, glorious sight our fearful eyes would then behold;
An empty grave and blazing light eclipsing warm, the stone so cold.

So let me walk with you, my Lord and feel your glorious presence now
As you just lay your piercèd hand upon my longing, loving brow.
It seems as if that I can hear that voice so sweet and tender to the ear:
Weep not, my child, I live, rejoice! Yes, he is risen, HE IS NOT HERE!

****

Rejoice, I'm working!

"Rejoice in the Lord always ..." Phil. 4:4a NIV

"Are not two sparrows sold for a penny?... don't be afraid; you are worth more than many sparrows." Matt. 10:29-31 NIV

Father, I give you all those things I have tried to control, even manipulate.
The circumstances I, with desperation –
Often with panic – have tried to stop from worsening.
With human effort and prayers of desperation,
Caught in the spiral of grief and unbelief.

I hear that command to the ruler Jairus
When he heard his little daughter had died,
And the natural mind would have said: It's too late --
There's nothing you can do now! But gazing into the broken
heart and face of that father, your Son said:
Be not afraid, only believe! I, too, hear him say that to me.

Opening my mind and my spirit to the blazing light of his Spirit,
Relinquishing those griefs and disappointments
I was holding so tightly within me.
Knowing that you are a God Who can be intreated,

Who is working out a marvellous plan Which I can't imagine
At this point in Time. You will bring to pass every word
You have spoken and placed in my heart.

Like Mary Magdalene at the tomb, I hear that voice say:
Woman, why do you cry? Places where Death has reigned
Shall be replaced with Life immortal.
The undisputable Truth of my Resurrection
Will take root in hearts waiting to be convinced,
Take root that *nothing* shall shake this personal knowing.

Those dear to you whose feet are wandering, stumbling
In the ways of sin and rebellion, will be confronted with me –
the Living Christ! I was able to turn around Saul of Tarsus
And make him Paul the Apostle, so shall I change the lives of
those running from me, I will heal their backslidings, love them
freely!

Therefore, rejoice and lift up your head!
In the unseen world I am working on every situation –
So rejoice, my daughter, and again I say
Rejoice!!

****

The Feast

The time of mourning has ended, my long-lost son has come again.
O, it's time to kill the fatted calf, go and get him out of the pen!
Reuben, you spread the table, Mary, bring out the choicest wine.
Joshua, fetch the best robe, a ring and sandals for this son of mine.
Call the minstrels and the harpist, those who make a joyful sound,
It's time for music and dancing, for my long-lost son at last is found!

****

There in your Desert

Choking burning sand
Barrenness, Isolation
Aloneness
Now just stripped to the bone
It would seem all is lost
Nothing left, you're bereft
When hot tears are long past
Your soul wrung out

**But you turn aside
With a listening ear –
There in your desert
I will speak to you!**

****

The Life-Mender

Out of Life's broken pieces he fashioned a vessel anew.
When others scoffed you are worthless, he said:
                        I've a plan just for you.
Jesus, he who was broken on Calvary's cross there for me,
Poured out his life-blood, to set broken ones like me, free!

He put the pieces so together, that one could really wonder
                        whether they had been broken at all.
With loving care he placed them there. Tender yet strong, his hands
working on and in my life. Asking for my trust when not
understanding, usually receiving only struggles and questions.

Flow, Holy Spirit, thro' the deepest recesses of my being and nature,
Make me according to the Father's plan. Teach me to mount up on

eagles' wings, over the broken things which surround me at present.
Teach me to turn my eyes upward to the Son, and build my shelter
in and upon the Rock –- Christ Jesus.
When the mighty winds blow, my nest will not be dislodged.
For I am hidden in the shelter of this eternal Rock.
I run into the Name of my Father, as into an impregnable fortress
As the tornado sweeps across my path –- and I am saved!
It sweeps on and past, but my soul is hidden in him.

My heart cries out for him, this my Saviour, Lover of my soul.
He draws me in unexplainable, inexplicable ways to his side.
No other place where I may hide; no other breast to lay my head
in such comfort; no other ear to hear my faintest whisper, my
scream in the darkness when it seemed all was lost I held so dear.
No other hands so capable of receiving all the broken pieces my
hands bring and place in them, knowing somewhere deep within me,
that as I draw near to him, he will draw near to me, and take me up.
His arms clasp me, like a warm blanket on a cold night;
Those arms and hands that flung galaxies of suns, stars into space,
Holding them in place by the Word of his power

Yet take broken children of Humanity, making them whole again.
Turning around our rejection and pain, accepting us with merciful
unconditional love --- just as we are. The Life-Mender who is
longing to change us, bringing our feet out of the net,
opening the iron doors and cages which hold us fast,
stepping out victorious and taking us with him --- **into freedom!!**

****

The Point of Contact

With weakened frame, tear-dimmed eyes I crossed the market square
'Twas filled with people hurrying by, excitement filled the air.
They jostled one another close, hurried, skipped and ran
Along a certain dusty road, then I remembered --- the Man
The Teacher come from Nazareth was to pass this way today.
He healed the sick, the maimed, I'd heard, and made the sad ones gay.
And my tired heart and weary breast took hope that One was here

To bring me health, peace, rest after suffering of twelve long year.
To many doctors I had been and made my faltering way,
A Jewess, I was called 'unclean' and shut off from society.

"O tell me, Sir, what's that you say, the Master's called away?"
"The ruler Jairus came for him, his daughter is dying today."
"He is my only hope!" I cried. A thought flashed thro' me then
Pushed through the crowd till by his side, I touched his garment hem.
And all at once new strength flowed in, my body was so strong!
The blood of Youth leapt in my veins, not felt for twelve years long!
The Master turned and in his face reigned Love, his eyes so rare,
Strength adorned by wondrous grace captured and transfixed me there.
"Who touched me, Daughter, was it you?" His voice dispelled my fears.
"Your faith has brought health to you. Be of good cheer, dry your
                                                                tears."
I'll always praise Jehovah-God and Jesus Christ his only Son
For bringing on that Summer day peace to this humble, seeking one!

****

They're waiting

Waiting on a distant shore, they've heard a little, want to know more
Of the God who gave his only Son for a world that's lost in sin, undone.
They're waiting still, won't you go and tell the story they need to know?

They're sitting there in squalor and dirt by huts of mud in fear and hurt.
Bound by chains of Satan's power, waiting for their deliverance-hour.
They're waiting still, won't you go and tell the story they need to know?

Standing at the corner of the street they sold themselves for sin so sweet
But now turned sour, they want to run — how to undo the sin they've done?
They're waiting still, won't you go and tell the story they need to know?

Trapped within a drug-addict's world, trips that spun, blazed and whirled
Now with arms full of needle-holes, death waiting to take all of their souls.
They're waiting still, won't you go and tell the story they need to know?

Sitting behind a polished desk, heads full of figures, problems grotesque.
Pockets full but no peace within, to cover their boredom an empty grin.

They're waiting still, won't you go and tell the story they need to know?

Living there in your neighbour's house, trapped like a cat with a mouse.
People you see every day in the town aimlessly walking up and down.
They're waiting still, won't YOU go and tell the story they need to know?

****

This is the Day of your Favour

This is the day of your favour, this is the day of your grace,
A day when you wonders will do to show forth Father's praise.
We shall go forth in his glory, sons of God thro' Jesus the Son
Taking light where darkness reigns, in your Name battles are won.

Prepare us for your visitation, we're expecting the rivers to flow,
Streams in our desert, rain on our nation, to the ends of the
                                      earth we will go.
Sensitive always to your Spirit, obedient to follow his voice
Rising in power for our finest hour, broken Church of Jesus ---
                                      rejoice!

Come now, sit at his table, drink the sparkling wine of his love
His blood now to cleanse you, his Spirit to refresh you
To fill you with life from above. This is the day of his favour
Yes, this is the day of his power; **rise up Church of God**
With hearts in one accord for this is the day of the Lord!!

****

"So if the Son sets you free, you will be free indeed!"
John 8:36 NIV

FREE! FREE! FREE!

      I thought the walls had closed around me,
      Depression dark had held me low.
      But oh, the door was standing open,

Twas only out I had to go!
A piercèd hand had come and broken
Every chain that held me fast,
Filled my dungeon with his presence,
Brought me into light at last.
You who are sitting in that shadow,
Rise up, take your deliverance now!
To Jesus Christ the mighty Conqueror,
Satan and his works must bow!!

****

To see yourself a Winner

To see yourself a winner, whilst still living in defeat.
To see yourself a winner, before you smell the victory sweet.
To see yourself a winner when it seems you're going down.
To see yourself a winner before you wear the winner's crown!

To see yourself a winner before the storms of Life have ceased,
To see yourself a living winner, not as one already gone ---
                              deceased!
To see yourself a winner, why just linger in despair,
To see yourself a winner, because JESUS is always there!

George Jesze

****

Walking through Meadow-Grass

Walking through meadow-grass
                Thinking about Jesus.

Lifting my arms to fleecy clouds, blue sky
                Loving Jesus.

Drinking at the mountain-spring
                Thanking Jesus.

Throwing a stone in a pool and casting my care
                Upon Jesus.

Leaving my Tomorrows to Him ---
                Trusting Jesus.

****

Who made the Flowers

Who made the flowers in my garden? Who made the sun up in the sky?
Who made birds to fly in the Heavens? Who made little boys like you and I?

Who put the horses in the meadow? Who gave me eyes so big and brown?

Who made the fishes in the river? Who made all the people in the town?

Who gave the whiskers to the pussy? Who put the conkers on the tree?
Who made the sand upon the seashore? Who made the seaweed in the sea?

**Jesus Christ, yes, Jesus did it. Jesus, the Son of God so fair.
Don't you know he made them all? Don't you know he loves them all?
Don't you know he cares?!**

(When our children were small, they and I wrote this poem!)

****

Wonderful Time in which to Live

Wonderful time in which to live, wonderful days when God doth give
Gifts unto men thro' the Holy Ghost, salvation thro' his Son whom
                                                          he loved the most.
Wonderful time in which to live --- Jesus is coming soon!
Troubles around, no peace can we see, nations fighting on land and sea,
Preparing their deadly weapons of war, destruction seems at the door.
Wonderful time in which to live --- Jesus is coming soon!

So many people crowd the earth, unwanted deaths, unwanted births.
Life over before twenty-one, tried it all, nothing more to be done.
Wonderful time in which to live --- Jesus is coming soon!
Famine stalks thro' the land anew, bloated stomachs, ribs showing thro'.
Earth quakes, houses fall, no place to run to, no safety at all!
Wonderful time in which to live --- Jesus is coming soon!

Falling the pound, the dollar, the mark. The future looks uncertain, dark.
Rising the prices, tighten the belt, for fear the hearts begin to melt.
Wonderful time in which to live --- Jesus is coming soon!
Flowers in December, snow in June, it seems that Nature's out of tune.
Weather proclaiming loud and clear the Day of the Lord is very near.
Wonderful time in which to live --- Jesus is coming soon!

In this time of fear and despair when it seems as if even God doesn't care,
Remember his plan, his timing is right. Our day will dawn --- for the

world –- the *night*.
Wonderful time in which to live --- JESUS IS COMING SOON!

****

Wrap me in your Presence

Wrap me in your presence, O my Father
Draw me, draw me closer now to you.
Let your presence permeate me, your Spirit now create me
To be the person that you want me to.
Wrap me in your presence, precious Jesus
Safe from every storm, the coldness of the world
For here I would abide, in your presence would I hide,
Trusting in the power of your Word!

****

"... God has said, never will I leave you; never will I forsake you... we say with confidence, The Lord is my helper; I will not be afraid. What can man do to me?" Hebrews 13:5b + 6 NIV

You're not Alone

You're not alone when you face the fiery furnace
You're not alone when you're in the lion's den.
You're not alone when it seems your heart is broken
He'll make you whole, cause you to sing again.
You're not alone when all around you crumbles
You're not alone when friends just turn away.
You're not alone when darkness closes round you
He'll change your world and turn your night to day.

For Jesus said, I'll never, never leave you
I'll not forsake my child who is so dear
On the Father's hand your name is clearly written
When you don't feel me still I am so near.

The Greater One, this Fourth Man in the fire
Will walk with you and shield you from the flame.
His love surrounds you that you will not feel
The heat, the scorch, there's power in his Name!

Peace like a river, peace like a river
You commanded, you demanded my peace be like a river.
Amid the storms and the thorns that wound my feet upon the pathway
You commanded and demanded Peace for me, peace for me.
And my peace is in you, Lord, not in the things around.
My peace is in you Lord, peace that nowhere can be found.
You are my Prince of Peace, and my Light, the Joy upon my way
My peace is in you, Lord, giving me faith and hope
For each new day, for each new day.

****

You'll still go on

When stars will fall like Autumn leaves, you'll still go on.
When Summer and Winter for ever cease, you'll not be gone.
When the sun has burned and scorched the earth
And Time to Eternity given birth,
You'll still be around, my friend, your spirit-life will never end
You'll still go on.

If the heavens shake with atomic power, you'll still go on.
When the devil has his final hour, you'll not be gone.
When men cry out for rocks to fall, too late on the Lord will call
You'll still be around my friend, your spirit-life will never end
You'll still go on.

When Armeggedon's battle rages you'll still go on.
When the Book of Life has closed its pages, you'll not be gone.
When men on horses, red, pale, black come out to ride,
                                                there's no turning back
You'll still be around my friend, your spirit-life will never end
You'll still go on.

When thousands stand at the great White Throne, you'll still go on.
When they'll be judged by God alone, you'll not be gone.
When the angel opens up to look if your name is in the Book
You'll still be around my friend, your spirit-life will never end,
Yes, in Heaven or Hell, my friend --- you'll still go on!

****

Somebody's here

Somebody's here with a broken heart, somebody's dream is broken.
Somebody's longing for a word of comfort to be spoken.
Somebody's heart is full of despair, their tears like rain are falling.
Somebody's arms are empty now, out in the dark they're calling:
Is there nobody there to help me? Isn't there anybody who cares?
Is there no-one who understands me? Can't anyone hear my prayer?

Somebody's here who can heal your heart and mend a life that's broken.
Somebody's here whose comforting words long since have been spoken.
Somebody's heart is full of love, he waits to dry your tears.
Somebody's arms are outstretched to you, to carry you through the years.
It is JESUS who is here to help you. It is JESUS who always cares.
He's the One who understands you, it's JESUS who has heard your prayer!

****

Under the Covering

Under the covering of his love all my doubts and fears
Covered up by his mercy those things that brought me tears.
His purity covers my stains as I sit there at his table
Under the covering of his love, through Jesus I am able
To stand before him as though I'd never sinned
Condemnation gone from me, for under the covering of his love

I am set free!

Under the covering of his blood shed on Calvary
Blood that poured from head and hands, his back, his side, his feet.
Blood-drops sweat in Gethsemane heal my mind and wounded soul.
In Christ I am a new creation, his Word renews and makes me whole.
And I stand before him as tho' I'd never sinned, condemnation gone from me,
For under the covering of his blood I AM SET FREE!

You washed away my every stain, you Lamb of Calvary.
You justified, just as if I'd never sinned or gone astray.
You are the wondrous Lord of love, bring me blessings from above
You are the One who gives me life – Lord Jesus Christ!

You are the One who gives me joy and heals my wounded soul
You are the One who comforts me and makes me new and whole.
You are the One who won my love, I worship you with all my heart
You are the One who fills my life – Lord Jesus Christ!

****

After the Storm

After the storm comes the calm, after the wound comes the balm.
After the tempest comes peace to my soul, after the sickness he makes me whole.
After the problems solutions I find, after confusion comes peace of mind.
In every trouble he sees my life, pours in his love to drive out the strife.
Gives me all that I need for my day, Jesus the Light, the Truth and the Way.
Do not despair, he's still there, JESUS, the Son of God!

****

New Sunrise

One day black darkness wrapped around me, I felt numb with despair.
I struggled through fog like a drunken man with nobody really to care.
My disappointments and my failures I had looked at far too long,
But then I heard the sweet strains of a song:

Sunset must give way to a new sunrise, deep in your heart let hope arise.
Your God's not dead he's still alive, and he will give you songs in the night.
And so I cried, Lord, please show me the next step out of this night.
Let me not walk round and round in circles, searching but missing the light.
I felt his loving hand upon me bringing comfort to my soul
And the power in his Word it made me whole!

Yes, he can heal broken hearts, turn water into wine.
He will give you love instead of hate, make everything just fine.
His plans for you are good ones, and with God your future's bright.
Be encouraged, friend, lift up your head tonight!
Sunset must give way to a new sunrise, deep in your heart let hope arise.
Your God's not dead, he's still alive and he will give you a new sunrise!

****

Hold me Steady

When troubles come my way, don't know how to face the day,
When it seems despair and sadness engulf me with their blackness.
There's no future and no hope and I'm at the end of my rope,
Help me Jesus, to look up and humbly say:
Hold me steady in the storm, Lord Jesus, when the waves beat on my boat
And I can hardly keep afloat.

Hold me steady in the storm, Lord Jesus, steady with the anchor of your Word.

When fear would grip my mind, all its tendrils round me bind
Keeping me in iron chains never to come out again.
When I don't know how to pray and there seems to be no way,
Help me Jesus, to rise up in your mighty Name!

Even in the prison-cell I know that you do all things well
And your promises to me are just like a special key
To unlock the gates of brass, bringing miracles to pass,
Giving me Lord Jesus, wondrous victory!!
You hold me steady in the storm, Lord Jesus,
Tho' the waves beat on my boat and I can hardly keep afloat.
You hold me steady in the storm, Lord Jesus,
Steady with the anchor of your Word!

****

Wondrous One

O you healer of broken hearts, O you healer of broken hearts,
O touch us now, you Wondrous One
O you healer of broken hearts.

O you healer of broken lives, O you healer of broken lives
O touch us now, you Wondrous One
O you healer of broken lives.

**So bring to him your broken pieces, so bring to him your broken life
So bring to him your broken pieces, bring them to him, he's the Lord of life.
And he will mend you, yes, he will mend you, you'll be surprised just what he'll do
Yes, he will mend you and he will heal you, for he loves you, yes, he loves you!**

****

Hiding in You

Lord, I'm hiding in you, till the storm is past you'll see me through
When the waters me surround and my feet can't touch the ground
Lord, I'm hiding in you.
When the sun is hidden from my sight and it seems my day has turned to night,
When I cannot understand, I'll just hold you by the hand,
Lord, I'm hiding in you!

Like a mighty fortress standing strong, when besieged I'll sing a victory song.
Like a bird that's hidden in the rock, a ship that's sheltered in the dock,
Lord, I'm hiding in you.
When the sun is hdden from my sight and it seems my day has turned to night,
When I cannot understand, I'll just hold you by the hand,
Lord, I'm hiding in you!

Lord, I'm hidden in you, now the storm is past, you've seen me through.
See, the water's going down, beneath my feet I feel the ground,
Lord, I'm hidden in you!
Gone away the darkness and the night, my horizon blazes with your light.
Once again you've shown that you, in every test will bring me through,
Lord, I'm hidden in you!!

****

To Live Again!

An empty space, where before the face
Of my loved one had been.

An empty heart through pain torn apart

Bleeding, broken, shattered.

An empty chair now just a cushion there
For he has gone who sat.

An empty hand groping for another hand
Now lifeless but once strong.

Empty arms that love once calmed
My longing to be held.

Empty thoughts, bleak, dark, pain-wrought
No future, hopeless.

My emptiness, come fill with loveliness
Lord, Master, Jesus Christ.

Destroy the thief of pain and grief
Bring healing, wholeness.

Love expanding you are. Now handing
A new love to accept.

**As you now fill my life and thrill
Me with love – I live, I live again!**

****

The Turning-Point

Candles flickering softly, glasses raised, women near invitingly
                                      --- waiting only for my wish.
The red walls seem to darken, rush upon me, closing me in.
I want to rush across the snow, fling to darkened skies my arms,
And cry for help. Thoughts and questions race through my brain
Like the wind-driven snow behind the pane. What had he said?
That old but oddly attractive-faced man I saw in the cafe?
I recall how he sat at my table, stirring a cup of pale frothed coffee
And said: Young man, Jesus Christ died to save you from your sins.

He loves you! Go to hell! I'd spat in his face. Then his answer:
I was on my way there, then I met this Jesus. Now he's making a
Place for me in Heaven. How about you?
I grab the wine and fill up again, grab the nearest waist, draw it near.
Eat, drink and be merry, for tomorrow we die.
There it is again --- die, Heaven, hell, my God!
I push her away in disgust. *What's wrong with me?*

The light has gleamed on chestnut hair in the corner of the room.
Her hair shone like that! Something stirs in my stomach, in my heart ---
 The memory of that tear-stained face, of my wife's face as I had
                                                    slammed out the door.
Drink, anything to push away that voice: DO NOT COMMIT
                                                    ADULTERY.
 Too late now, she would never have me back. AND GOD?
 Spurning *his* love is worse than trampling *her* love
 Underfoot. No, not tonight, chick, another time.

I head for the door; cold air hits and sobers me. Slam in the car-key ---
Wait a minute, don't drink and drive!
 Walk under that sky, snow crunching underfoot. Are you there, God?
Jesus? Is it true? What was that story – The Prodigal Son, they called it.
Yes, that's me; but O, the loneliness, is it worth it, running away from
                                                    Him?
How quiet it is and quietness is spreading within me.
Almost peace you could call it, I've never known peace.
Sit on this log, head buried in hands:
 If you're there, unknown God and Saviour Jesus Christ,
Take me out of this rotten mess of my life and make me a son of
                                                    yours!

                           ****

Now Winter's here!

Rust on reeds and frost on grass, cold, stiff, white as by we pass.
The river sheens with an icy coat, early robin with red chest-throat.
The air is still, Nature's asleep, ancient hills their watch do keep.
Bare trees reach to heavens above stretch up to the God of Love.
Hurry home to fire's warm heat, toast our muffins, toast our feet
Lean back in our chair with friends held dear and chat till Spring –
  now Winter's here!

****

Stories in Rhyme

Old-fashioned Ballad of Love

An old man stood at his garden-gate, looking down a country lane
He looked for a well-known face he loved, many a year in vain;
For Bill his son had gone to sea and left the old home behind
For the song of the sea, of foreign ports and adventure had
                                              filled his mind.
His step grew slow and his hair turned white, waiting every day.
And many a tear was shed in the house since Bill had gone away.
And brown-eyed Mary she waited long, and many a time said 'No'
When others asked for her hand, for Bill had told her he loved her so.
Down on the bridge, o'er the rushing stream, he'd said: Will you wait
                                               for me?
And she said: I'll wait tho' the time be long while you are gone to sea.

+++++++

Well, where is Bill all this long time? --- Behind dark prison bars,
With grey stone walls, a bed of straw, and a view of sky or stars.
All the temptations of a seaman's life had turned him to the bad
And practised hands had tricked and deceived the weak-willed
                                               country lad.
One day, Bill sat in dejection and gloom, looking down at the floor
When he heard footsteps approaching and a key turned in the door.
It was the chaplain with greying hair and shrewd but kindly face
Who came to visit, to have a chat, and tell of the Saviour's grace.
Then as he read in Luke fifteen about the Prodigal Son,
Bill said it fitted his story well like none other could have done.

But it's too late now, Sir, he cried. I think it's too late for me!
Never too late, the Father waits and Jesus will set you free!
Then as they knelt on the bare stone floor God's power came
                                             in that cell,

Made a new creature out of Bill, gave him fresh hope as well!

+++++++

O Mother, look here! The old man cried. A letter from our Bill.
He wants to know if we forgive and if we love him still!
Imagine their rejoicing in the cottage kitchen there, thanking the
                            Heavenly Father for the answer to their prayer!
The old man went in the garden and made everything just right.
All must be looking spick and span --- Bill was to come that night!
The mother cleaned and prepared Bill's room and put plants on
                                        the window-sill,
Then sent a message to Mary in the cottage over the hill.
The old man stood at his garden-gate and looked down the
                                        country lane,
And he looked for a well-known face he loved, but *this* time,
                                                not in vain!
And the Heavenly Father is waiting still for all who have gone astray,
Saying with loving, tender voice: O won't *you* come home, *today?!*

****

The Farmer

I'd like to have a harvest, the farmer said one day
So he went and looked at his fields down along the way.
Well, you'd better plant some seed, his wife then she said.
O no, the Lord will do it all! And off he went to bed!
And so he daily dreamed about a golden harvest fair.
He then told all his neighbours: You'll see it standing there.
But he never took the trouble even once to plough the land
And he never sowed any seed from his foolish hand.

He said: My God he is so great, there's nothing he can't do,
He's promised seedtime and harvest and I shall see it too!
Well, the weeks grew into months, the months grew into years
But still there was no harvest, no grain, no golden ears.
Now before you laugh at this old man who didn't sow any seed
Ask yourself the question: Haven't you got any needs,
And you sit there wondering why the answer doesn't come,

Why the Lord doesn't answer you, why the thing isn't done?

Why your finances are so low and the problems are there still,
Why your family's still unsaved or you're still sick and ill?
Have you been sowing the devil's seed of worry, fear and doubt
Then expected a harvest of blessing will one day come about?
It never did work in the past and it won't work today.
For if you want God's blessings, you must do things in God's way.
So throw away the devil's seed and use the Lord's instead.
Plant it deep in your spirit, it will bring forth, he's said.

With faith and patience you will see the promises come true
God's law of sowing and reaping, and it will work for YOU!

****

Fisherman's Daughter

Fisherman's Daughter leaves footprints on firm wet sand.
Her black skirt blows in the stiff breeze as she runs along.
Seagulls wheel and call, sky blue, laced with fleecy clouds.
She stops, gazes out to sea, her deep blue eyes hold fear.
Fishermen's Daughters have fear their men will not return

On stormy nights when waves roar like hungry monsters
And the warning-beacon is lit, and the fishermen struggle
To keep their boats from dashing to pieces on the rocks ---
Fear that the ones they love will never return to their arms.
Fisherman's Daughter shudders, pulls her home-spun shawl
Round her shapely shoulders, runs to meet Fisherman's Son.
Waiting behind the lighthouse, he looks eagerly for his love.
Fear gone in joy of meeting, so proud of Fisherman's Son.
Sees the strength in his broad shoulders and chest ----
Laughs at his slow-spoken Cornish speech, rose-pink
Blushes at the love in his eyes, the longing in his kiss.
Fisherman's Daughter will wait.

Fisherman's Son is preparing their humble cottage,
She is spinning and sewing for their wedding-day.
He longs to say how beautiful she is in her bodice and shawl,
Browned skin, a few curls peeping out from the head-scarf;
But he is Fisherman's Son, a man of few words, used to dark
Lonely hours on the sea --- and his tongue refuses to say it.
Fisherman's Son and Fisherman's Daughter meet in the cove,

By the lobster-pots, up on the chalk cliff where the gulls nest,
In the harbour, down at the fish-market as he sells his wares.
Fisherman's Daughter is restless. Like the waves of the sea,
Ever searching, ever moving. Wonders if she is just like
A pebble washed up by the tide of Life, with so many others
Pushed, jostled relentlessly with no power of its own
To withstand or shape its circumstances. Wonders Who made
The regular ebb and flow of the tides, brilliance of sunrise
And sunset, gold, pink, orange. Did He make her too?
Fisherman's Daughter goes to the wooden mission-hall down
At the harbour, hears preacher tell of One who made all things,
Who created her, and His Son who said to Fishermen's Sons,
"Come, follow me, I will make you Fishers of MEN",
Of the One who stilled the storm and said so often, "Fear not".
Fisherman's Daughter is satisfied. Kneels at crude altar-bench.
Leaves her sin and fear at His cross. And follows.
Fisherman's Son, too.

****

Red-Shoes

Just a little woman walking down the street,
Just a little woman, red shoes on her feet.
Bought them at the market, thinks she owns the world
Make-up to perfection, black hair blow-dry curled.
Just a little woman walking straight and strong,
Just a little woman clicking all along.
Got a job at *Nightmare,* the flashy corner-club.
'Twas them shoes that did it, said Rico at the pub.

Just a little woman dancing down the street
Just a little woman, red shoes on her feet.
Living now with Charlie – Charlie's love is wild.
But Charlie doesn't know she's carrying his child.
Just a little woman coming down the street.
Just a little woman like any you could meet.
Got a brood of children and a black eye, too,
Where Charlie went and hit her that morning in the loo.

Just a little woman reeling down the street
Hair messed up, eyes all glazed, red shoes on her feet.
Got myself a Blue-shoes! said Charlie and was gone.
Drink and drugs now fill her life – can't bear to be alone.
Just a little woman at the corner of the street,
Trying to pick up clients, red shoes on her feet.
No-one wants to have her. You're too old! they cry.
Tracy laughs, swings her hips, the car goes crawling by.

Just a little woman tottering down the street
Two o'clock in the morning and no-one there to meet.
Swirls of fog surround her, in her face despair
Pulls her thin coat round her, freezing cold night air.
He saw it in the paper, it gave him quite a start,
But he laughed it off with Green-Shoes for Charlie had no heart.
First they found her red shoes by the river-side,
Later on, her body floating on the tide.

" … the Son of Man is come to save that which was lost."
Matthew 18:11 KJV
****

The Vicar

Down in the hole of tradition he'd preached and pastored for years.
He'd kept to his creed and his doctrine, no place for emotion or tears.
He'd prided himself on his logic and all his professors had taught,
He'd christened, married and buried, done all he thought that he ought.
Casting out devils and healing were words he didn't like said,
And he always squirmed uncomfortably when the end of Mark
                                                sixteen was read.
And as for the gifts of the Spirit, why, the FRUITS are much better,
                                                you know,
Speaking in tongues and prophecy — he didn't like *that* kind of a show.
Yet it was most disturbing, he thought as he sat in his chair,
These reports of strange goings-on in churches and groups everywhere.
Not just a few odd fanatics you'd dismiss with a wave of your hand,
But some of the church's own 'faithful' were visiting the heretic band!
They talked of the Spirit's outpouring, that God is at work here today!
And anything more preposterous he'd never heard anyone say!
With faces alight they had told him that his very own Deacon Jones
Was healed in a charismatic meeting of lumbago and kidney-stones!
But now the worst thing that could happen, was Annetta his wife
Had gone to another meeting and said she had found there new life!
Sometimes coming home he found her down on her knees by the bed,
Reading her Bible or listening to tapes as if she'd gone out of her head!
He asked for a short explanation, laughing, she said: Don't you know?
It's only the work of God's Spirit that Joel talked about long ago.

Now he was faced with a challenge and a problem, what was he to do?
For here on his very own doorstep were things he'd considered taboo!
He could see on his parish horizon a cloud now coming his way
But if it held trouble or blessing, he couldn't at this point, quite say!
Wearied he took his black Bible, cherished and well-used with age,
And tho' he didn't know where to look "Acts 2:4" stood out on the page.
A cry came from his heart as he sat there: O Lord, please show to me
If there's something that I should know which I didn't learn in seminary!
The telephone rang and he started, then felt the sweat on his brow,
For wasn't it inconvenient someone should ring up just now!
"Praise the Lord!" an exuberant voice on the line ---
('Twas that awful preacher he'd met who had asked if he knew of the
                                                'move of God'

And 'your's truly' had told him to --- GET!)
"I'd like to call and have a chat at four o'clock today
For I'm preaching in your area and shall be coming your way."
And Annetta outside the study, she danced a jig with glee
For he'd told her who was coming and to make a pot of tea!

And of course, you know how it ended, for our vicar opened his heart
And asked the Saviour to be Lord of his life, of ALL, not just a part.
Well, they talked right into the evening and before the clock struck nine
He was filled with the Spirit, speaking in tongues, overflowing with
                                              God's new wine.
Of course, there were some didn't like it and said that hmmm ---
                                              the bishop should know!
But the numbers increased and the church was so blessed
That they couldn't really tell him to go!
And so there are similar stories all over the world now, you know
For God is seeking a people who with him the *whole* way will go.
Equipped with the Word and the Spirit and a heart full of God's love,
Who want God the Father, and Jesus the Son ---
And make room for the Heavenly Dove!

                  ****

Ode to Pentecostals

I want to tell you a story of several years ago
My neighbour took me down the road to her little church,
                                              you know.
It seemed so strange, I wondered what it was all about,
They clapped their hands when singing, some did even shout!
They called it *Pentecostal* --- to me that was absurd!
They said it was in the Bible but I'd never heard the word!
And yet they seemed so happy and were friendly to me there,
It did my lonely heart some good, like a breath of real fresh air.

I remember well, one Sunday night the Pastor preached on Love,
The love of God who sent his Son to earth from Heaven above.
And all at once I felt a tear come trickling down my face

I wanted Jesus in my heart and to know his saving grace.
I became a child of God that night, the bells of Heaven rang
With joy over my repentance and I'm sure the angels sang.
I thought my vicar would be glad but he gave me such a stare
And said I was fanatical like that crazy lot down there!
He said they claimed to speak in tongues like in Acts chapter 2,
And if I wanted to go there, I'd soon be doing it too!

Well, one day I was singing and making myself some toast
When Jesus came and baptised me in his wonderful Holy Ghost!
And then I began to witness and to read the Bible more
And I had a love for Jesus I had never had before.
Such wonderful days of blessing, souls saved every week,
And healings, you should have seen them! And how our Pastor
                                                                         could speak!
How I long for the good old days with Brothers like Donald Gee
Who came to speak at conventions and at the Fellowship Tea.
We've prayed for years for revival but it doesn't seem to be here,
Sometimes no power in the meetings and many an empty chair.
Our church is new and modern, the old hall went long ago,
We've a college-trained young pastor, but there's no room for the
                                                                            Spirit to flow.
Two hymns, a prayer and the offering, with notices number three,
The choir and then the sermon and home to look at TV!
For a new generation has arisen that doesn't know God's power.
I may be old and unlearnèd, but I know it's the midnight hour!
We called ourselves Pentecostal, thought other churches were dead
But it seems that they are coming alive for the other day I read
Of the Holy Ghost's outpouring on Christians far and near,
And that new vicar at St. Mark's is filled with the Spirit, I hear!

Smith Wigglesworth gave a prophecy in Africa to Du Plessis
That this was going to happen and he'd play a large part, you see.
It seems that we Pentecostals have had our head in the sand
And haven't seen what God is doing, up and down the land.
At first the churches didn't want us because we stood out square
For *all* the Bible, not just the part they were preaching here and
                                                                                 there.
But now the time has come to *forgive* as the Lord's forgiven *us*
For if we don't, then we shall find that we have missed the bus!

For the Lord is marching onwards and to me it's very clear
He's calling us into a new thing now and some are not ready, I fear.
If we build a fence round the Spirit he won't have that at all!
One day we'll find he's no longer there, he's just jumped over the
                                                                        wall!
A Bride, the Spirit's preparing from every people on Earth,
From every church, whatever the name, as long as they've had the
                                                                        New Birth.

And so, dear Pentecostal friends, I challenge you today
To let the Lord renew your vision --- *give the Holy Ghost*
                                                                   right-of-way!

                                          ****

The Old Man

I saw the old man leave his house, pass thro' the rusty gate,
A shopping-bag in his feeble hand, they say he's eighty-eight!
And he looked so old and careworn, I felt I had to say
Is there anything I can do to help? And pass the time of day.
I asked him in for a cup of tea and a cosy little chat.
He warmed his feet by the fire, stroking my old black cat.
It's six years now since Annie died, the children are all gone.
The house seems very empty now, it's hard to be alone.

He fumbled for a handkerchief, the weak voice died away.
I poured him a second cup of tea and then went on to say:
Yes, loneliness is terrible but there's One who understands,
He waits to love you and fill your life, waiting with
                                                        outstretched hands.
Your Annie loved him, for she said she was going where
Sorrow or pain never came, to our heavenly home up there.
She was ready to go, and her heart was cleansed in the
                                                Saviour's precious blood.
What about *you?* If he called today, are you ready
                                                    to meet your God?

The clock ticked on, it was very quiet; Time ran into Eternity.

At last he said: You know I'm not, I'm not ready, pray for me!
Whoever calls on the Name of the Lord I will not turn away,
But I'll forgive and take him in, Jesus himself, did say.
Behold, I stand at the door and knock, if any man hears my voice
I will come in to have fellowship, so make God now your choice!
We prayed and the old man then looked up, a new light in his eye.
Thank you, my dear, what a help you've been, I'll see
Annie bye and bye.

Next day I heard the Lord had come and taken him home that night.
How glad I was I'd taken the time to show him the way that is right!
Loneliness is a terrible thing, but there's One who understands.
He waits for YOU, to fill your life, waiting with outstretched hands!

****

"... I went down to the potter's house, behold, he wrought a work on the wheel..."
Jeremiah 18, 3

The Plan

He sketched the blueprint with straight, clear lines, then a curve
And downward sweep, but I couldn't wait, spoiled his thoughts,
Crushed the plan and then did weep like a child so eager breaks
A toy, I took that precious thing called Life that He had given
And tried to make it come MY way.
So patient, there he stood, like a lamb before the slaughter, still,
With eyes so full of love he gazed at me; I turned away, I did not
Want to do his Will. Unlike a puppet, he had made me a person
Who could make a choice of going *my* path or obeying *his* voice.
My prodigal feet trod flower-strewn ways but even as I passed
They turned to dust, and demon faces mocked behind the gaily-
Painted tent, as on this restless quest my feet I bent.

He called me, loudly at first, as the days went by it fainter grew
For he was on the path and I had wandered --- grown deaf, too.
But as I plucked the fruit it was so bitter to my taste.
The sparkling stream from which I drank surely must have been
Filled with all the waste of rottenness.
No good for God, no good for the world, better to be cold or hot!

I heard the preacher cry, "Are you ready if he comes today?"
And I was not.

One day upon this rocky path enemies leapt out at me.
I'd lost my sword, the Word of God, and couldn't get the victory.
Wounded, crushed I lay in the dust, suddenly I heard my name.

He was searching, was yearning for me --- Love just the same.
His kingly robe and sandalled foot stumbled upon me there.
Submitting to his loving touch, I knew I had missed it much,
His beauty rare.

Stopping by the Potter's House; he put me on that fateful wheel
Broken and marred, his hand did feel and melt and mould and turn
Till a new shape began to take place; the blueprint of his design
Was better far than any of mine, I could only praise his grace.

Lie still in the hand that was marred for you,
Walk behind those wounded feet.
Let your heart beat in one with that of God's Son,
Till the day your Saviour you meet.

****

Inspirationals.

A Merry Heart!!
by George Jesze

"A merry heart doeth good like a medicine: but a broken spirit drieth the bones." Proverbs 17:22 KJV

Have you heard of that powerful international ministry some people have? It's called – the Ministry of Discouragement! And the devil sees to it that it never dies out!

We are told that when we smile we use 14 muscles in our face, and when we frown we use 72. So let's smile and be an energy-saver!

Has your God gone into recession? Can you imagine Jesus saying: Father, what are we going to do? We'll have to sell the pearly gates!

Have you had a pity-party lately? Elijah had one but his only problem was, he didn't have at least one spectator. We lap up self-pity, you know like if somebody says: O Sister Jones, you look so pale tonight! And it sort of does you good!

When God brings two people together, one is fiery and the other is cool. If both were fiery, you'd have a smashing time, flying saucers in the kitchen!

Some of you are no longer an amateur worrier but a professional.

Let God at least degrade you to an amateur-status, but better still, right out of the worry business altogether!

Some people are afraid of spiders. I've got good news for you – the spider is more afraid of you! You're a giant in his eyes! And if you only knew it, the devil is more afraid of you than you are of him, because of Jesus in you!

Are you a **worrier** or a **warrior**?! One letter which makes such a difference!

A man said to me he and his wife had been married for 50 years and had never had a cross word! I replied, Brother, what are you doing here? You should already be walking the golden streets – you're so perfect!

We're always blaming someone else for our mistakes. Do you know where we got that from? First Adam said, It's not me, Lord, it was the woman you gave me! Then Eve said to the serpent, It's your fault – and the trouble was the serpent had no-one else to blame!

Don't cry over spilt milk – get up and catch the cow! She's got some more!

The greatest distance is not from the earth to the moon, but from the head to the heart, what we know in theory before it gets down into our spirit. A lady said it took her thirty years – my, that's pretty slow travelling!

There should be a health warning: "Worry is detrimental to your health; it can even kill you." signed The Creator

God's medicine has no bad side-effects.

If we could re-educate the bull to know who his real enemy is – the matador, not the cloak he's holding -- bull-fighting days would soon be over! And if Christians would realise their real enemy is the devil and not their Brother or Sister in Christ, they would stop fighting each other.

Take your eyes off the problems and put them on His promises!

Perhaps we should make a bumper-sticker: Have you blessed your *stinker* today?! Or don't you have any? I've got a few! But God says "Forgive!"

The bed is a very dangerous place. More people die in bed than on the roads!

It's getting more expensive to live and more expensive to die. You can't afford a funeral yet, so keep on living!

Why did Moses have to spend 40 years in the wilderness? Because God couldn't prepare him in 39! It's not how long we've been in God's school, it's what we've learned!

We could rent Wembley Stadium for an International Christian Worry Olympics. Some of us would stand a good chance of getting a gold-medal every time!

Some people are wondering if the government will have enough money to pay their old-age pension. The way you're carrying on, you won't need a pension at all! You'll have worried yourself into your grave. What a waste of good money!

The storms of Life don't send you a postcard to tell you they're coming!

Forgiveness is like a boomerang; send it out and it'll come back to you.

It's OK to have a problem, but it's KO if the problem has you!

Some people are waiting for their ship to come home, but they haven't sent it out yet!

When the devil took everything from Job, he left him his wife. It was the straw that broke the camel's back when she said: Curse God and die!

One of the blessings of being married is, you've always got someone to blame!

If Jesus said to Peter after he had walked on the water "man of little faith", what would he say to us?!

Some people you'd like to hold a little longer under the water when they're being baptised, so the 'old man' really dies!

****

Well, I hope you have enjoyed and been blessed by these humorous quips and spiritual truths from George! A merry heart does us all good – "the joy of the Lord is our strength!"

****

A Refuge like None Other!!

"Therefore will not we fear, though the earth be removed, and though the mountains be carried into the midst of the sea ... Be still and know that I am God; ... The Lord of Hosts is with us; the God of Jacob is our refuge." Psalm 46:1,2,10a,11

"The eternal God is thy refuge and underneath are the everlasting arms." Deut. 33:27a

These verses have been ringing in my spirit this week. Many times in our lives we need a refuge; it may be mental, emotional, spiritual or even a physical refuge we need. A refuge is a protection, a shelter from danger or hardship. A place providing protection, a haven or sanctuary. Anything to which one may turn for help, relief or escape.

David the Shepherd Boy, later to become the king of Israel, wrote this Psalm. Hounded and chased for years by King Saul, he had so often needed a refuge, and through personal experience, he could say that GOD had been his greatest refuge. God had been a *present help,* a help when he had needed it, not just a help promised years ahead, but God had so often heard his cry and stepped in, giving him victory. I am sure that many of us can say the same thing, that God has been our refuge, our strong tower, our arm of protection, and when we have been weak, vulnerable, sick or in grief, we have felt those everlasting arms holding us up, as Moses wrote in Deuteronomy.

I wonder why David wrote about the earth shaking, waters roaring and mountains being moved. Perhaps he was speaking prophetically of what would often happen in the world, earthquakes and floods, Tsunamis, for although there had been Noah's flood, the Bible does not tell us that there had been any earthquakes which he would know about. We are clearly told that in *"The Last Days"* there will be an increase of ecological catastrophies. Watching the *News* this week, with over 9000 people dying in floods in Libya where storm *Daniel* has ravaged their country, or the earthquakes in Morocco and Turkey are just some recent examples.

He describes God as The Lord of Hosts, the Great One who will lead his armies to victory, overcoming every enemy. He also reminds God of His Covenant with His People Israel, when he calls Him "the God of Jacob". Just as God has made a Covenant with the physical nation of Israel, He has also made a Blood Covenant with his Church today – the born-again Believers worldwide, because of what his Son, Jesus, did on the cross of Calvary.

I do not know what your situation is today. Everything may be going along just wonderfully, or you may be in great difficulty and need a *refuge* to hide in. If you find yourself in that position like David, run into God your refuge! The arms of your Lord are open wide to receive you! Hide in Him today!

Moses reminds us that He is the "Eternal God" . Hebrews 13:8 tells us – "Jesus Christ the same, yesterday, today and forever." So we know the promise stands true today, for He is the Unchanging One. He will be the mighty strength which we need, hiding us until every storm is past! You can experience it again right now!

****

A Speaking God

When I first read the life-story of Helen Keller, a young woman who had become blind and deaf through an illness, at about two years old, I was deeply moved. The only means of communication she had with the world around her, was through touch and feeling vibrations. As she grew older, her frustration and anger grew, but it seemed nothing could unlock the cage, pierce the darkness –- that is, until her teacher, Anne Sullivan arrived. The breakthrough came when Anne held Helen's hand under a stream of water, and spelled the letters "w-a-t-e-r" into her hand. Suddenly, Helen realized that the cool freshness running over her fingers, had a name –- *water*. From this time, her world was changed. Helen went on to become an accomplished, studied woman, and a brilliant writer and speaker.

Before we know Jesus, we are blind and deaf like Helen, but *spiritually*. God is constantly seeking to communicate with the people in his world, drawing them to himself. He speaks through Nature and many other things. Two people may be talking, but they may not be *communicating*. They may not be understanding at all what the other is saying or feeling. God wants to speak to us today and bring a message. He may use some unusual methods. Let's listen with an open heart and an unprejudiced understanding.

He longs to communicate with us, for our God is a speaking and a hearing God!

****

An Attitude of Gratitude!

"Oh give thanks to the LORD, for he is good, for his steadfast love endures forever!" Psalm 107:1 ESV

"He shall not fail nor be discouraged, till he have set judgment in the earth: and the isles shall wait for his law," Isaiah 42:4 KJV

A legend says that a man found the barn where Satan kept all the seeds he sows into the hearts of men and women. More than any others, were seeds of **discouragement**. "But," he told the man, "there is one type of heart where this seed does not easily take root." "Oh, what is that?" asked the man. Satan answered, **"A grateful heart!"**

The Bible is full of verses telling us to give thanks and to praise God for all his mercies. Here the Psalmist encourages us to give thanks to God for "he is good, and his steadfast love endures forever". When we are discouraged we think of our problems, our needs, what we *don't have* and what we think we *should have.* People and Satan may tell us we will never amount to anything, we have nothing to offer, we have made too many mistakes and *how could God forgive us again* for the same thing?! Our eyes, heart and thoughts are fixed and focused on the negative, instead of remembering that we do not serve a *person,* but we serve an Almighty God whose very essence is LOVE; a God who gave the very best that he had to save us from our sins and set us free — his Son Jesus Christ, so how much more will he not, with him, freely give us all things!

When the armies of the Philistines had burned down the city of Ziklag and captured all the wives and children, David's men even wanted to stone him. But we read that David "encouraged and strengthened himself in the Lord". He remembered the sure mercies of his God in the Past, and that they were just as sure *that very day, in the Present!* He threw off discouragement, he and his men rode after the Philistines, overcame them and set free all their captive families!

An **Attitude of Gratitude** comes from a heart centred on Jesus, remembering those thousand and one mercies he has shown to us, and that he is *steadfast,* not a fair weather friend, but will be so in the Future as well. It has been said that "Our Attitude determines our Altitude".The altitude tells you how high or how low you are on the mountain. An Attitude of Gratitude will take us higher in God, will cause us to develop and grow in our Christian walk and relationship with Jesus.

The above verse in Isaiah is talking about "The Suffering Servant" who was to come, Jesus our Redeemer, and says that he will "not fail nor be discouraged", until he has accomplished all he set out to do. I am sure that Jesus, as the Son of Man, could have often been discouraged at the wickedness, suffering, opposition he encountered, but Jesus, the Son of God, saw *further* than that, fulfilling the will of his Father and did not fail or get discouraged.

My late husband, George, used to say, **"There are many people with the 'ministry of discouragement' and Satan sees to it that this 'ministry' never dies out!"** I am sure that every one of us does not want to have this 'ministry'! Instead, let's seek to have the **"ministry of encouragement"** to those around us, and even if we are in adverse circumstances at the moment, with the Lord's help, let's start developing that Attitude of Gratitude, and see him move on our behalf!

****

Behold, I will allure Her...

"Therefore, I will allure her, and bring her into the wilderness, and speak comfortably to her." Hosea 2:14 KJV

At some time in our lives, we will have a taste of the wilderness or desert. I've been there many times! There are several reasons why we might go into a 'wilderness' time or experience. One of these reasons is *Disobedience*. Hosea, the Prophet, was told by God to marry a prostitute. His marriage to Gomer was to show the nation of Israel that they had committed spiritual adultery and whoredoms by following other gods, but that nevertheless, God wanted to betroth himself to them forever and purify them.

Gomer was faithful for a while, but later returned to her old ways, like God's people. Hosea bought back his wife from the slave-market and in this context, God spoke of alluring the faithless bride, Israel, into the wilderness, that he might speak to her and change her. He promised to give her hope and to restore the song she used to sing in her youth, when she was brought out of Egypt, the land of bondage. Stripping her of all the things which were precious to her, there would only be her and God. He yearned to show her his heart and develop a heart-relationship.

This reminds us of the occasions when God removes our comfort and outward trappings, the crutches we leaned on, whether people or things, just as the mother eagle pecks out the soft lining, exposing the bare, thorny branches of the nest, then takes her baby and stands him on the edge of the rock. The eaglet is suddenly exposed to the winds, terrified and alone. Then Mother-eagle tips him over the cliff, and he's falling, falling...A fast-beating heart, sharp rocks below to kill, but Mum swoops down and catches him on her wings. She's teaching him to fly!

God often uses the same method to bring us to maturity. Taking us out of our comfort zone and a safe environment, he puts us in a position where it's only him and us, personally. This can be likened to a desert-experience, but in that very place, he speaks to us, shows us his heart, our life, his plans and preparation for the next steps, to bring us to the fulness of our stature in Christ, and fruition.

Jesus, standing in Jordan, dripping from his baptism, the Dove of the Holy Spirit coming upon him, God's voice openly pronouncing him as his Son, right at the commencement of his ministry, was led into the wilderness. There, tested by Satan, he overcame with the Word and returned "in the power of the Spirit".

Let's turn aside in our desert, and let him speak "comfortably" to us today.
He can cause it to blossom as the rose!

****

Dad's Old Saw

' "My son, do not make light of the Lord's discipline, and do not lose heart when he rebukes you, because the Lord disciplines those he loves...". No discipline seems pleasant at the time, but painful. Later on, however, it produces a harvest of righteousness and peace for those who have been trained by it.' Heb. 12:6+11 NIV

Every one of us who have accepted Jesus as their personal Saviour, has been called to follow him and be his "disciple". It was not just a one-time decision and then we forgot about it. We entered into a covenant-relationship with him; the next step after accepting Salvation was to make him our "Lord". This brings us into another stage of our spiritual development -- learning to become his "disciple". The words "disciple" and "discipline" belong together. Our Bible verses above show that sometimes God has to discipline us when he is training us, something we don't enjoy at all, but later, it produces good results.

I read a story by Mabel Marvin, which illustrates this well. Her father was a furniture maker. One day she went with him to buy a new saw, and he was very particular which one he bought. At last he was satisfied, and explained the steel of the chosen one had been tempered just right. This one would outlast all others and help him to make excellent furniture. Mr Marvin used that saw for many years. When old and sick and unable to work, he sold most of his tools, but gave this special saw to his daughter, so it would remain in the family.

Mabel and her husband, Henry, moved several times and the saw always went with them, although it was never used. One night an evangelist came to their church and he played on a musical saw. Her husband was fascinated and asked where he could buy a saw like that, as he would also like to learn to play. However, when Henry tried to buy one, he was very disappointed to find this brand was no longer being sold. Then Mabel had the bright idea of getting out her father's old saw. It was rusty, pitted and battle-scarred, but she explained that she had been with her father when he bought it and he said it was the best!

Henry decided to clean it up, so every evening he went to work with sandpaper, steel wool, a whetstone and oil. Then he had a pleasant surprise; under all the scars was the brand name -- the exact one he had been looking for! The next night he brought home a bottle of alcohol and some rosin. After applying them, he took the violin bow and drew it softly across the old saw. Music as high and vibrant as that of the evangelist's saw came forth! It had been worth his hard work!

Sometimes our life is like the old saw. When the Lord saved us he stamped "Christian" on us, seeing in us a tool of the finest steel. Just as steel has to be tempered by extreme heat and tested, so our Lord brings and allows tests and situations along our path to develop and strengthen our character, and mould us to his image. If our life was always a bed of roses, we would become lazy, indifferent, weak, drifting along, thinking we are well able to get on without Jesus. But when the difficulties come and there's nowhere else to turn, then we learn to cling onto our Saviour. We study his Word to find answers; we learn to pray as never before!

Just as Mr Marvin wanted a saw that would last for many years, so our God builds and prepares us, not just for the time on this Earth, but *for Eternity!* The old saw was laid aside for a long time, seemingly neglected and not fulfilling its purpose. Some characters in the Bible were like this. Joseph, lied about and put in prison; Moses, tending sheep in the back side of the desert; David, anointed to be King, yet hiding for years from his enemy, Saul. Although painful at the time, it did not harm these men. When God was finished with them, they became men of immense character who fulfilled a mighty purpose in his plan.

Perhaps you have felt left on the shelf, stuck in a corner, not knowing how to find your place. Or perhaps it seems that your talents are being wasted, that no-one recognises your potential and the ministry you could fulfil. Have Life and people left you scarred and rusted, and you feel you are no use to the Lord? These are times when we can become bitter or better, by submitting and letting him work on us with his spiritual sandpaper and 'tools'. These 'tools' may take many forms. We may be unjustly criticised, and it would be so easy to try to defend ourselves and chafe under the treatment we have received, or the promotion we were promised is cancelled, and all our plans are brought to nothing. Just as the oil gives the steel the final polish and the saw a truer ring, after the cleaning, God has his ways of doing that too.

So take courage, dear friend today, our Father knows just where

we are! Moses was kept in the desert for 40 years because he wasn't ready in 39 years, to fulfil the task God would be calling him to! Our Bible verse assures us that after the time of testing, good fruit and a rich harvest will be produced in our lives. We shall come forth, step out of our limitations, to shine and sing, making music for the King of kings!

****

Do not remember the former Things

"Do not remember the former things, neither consider the things of old. Behold I will do a new thing ..." Isaiah 43:18-19

On the last day of the old year we watched a television program, entitled: "Service for the Turning of the Year." It was broadcast from a church in Belfast. Behind the pulpit on the wall hung a plain wooden cross, with the word "Shalom" painted on the wall, next to it. This Hebrew word means peace and wholeness, and is used as a greeting in Israel. Here, it was not just a word, but a heartfelt prayer, for the city had seen much violence, and one nearby mission had been bombed thirty-four times!

We thought how fitting that the theme of the service was "God of New Beginnings". It meant new beginnings for war-torn Ireland, for families and communities torn apart, confused loyalties; new beginnings for those viewing and for everyone.

The New Year was about to begin and, like many other people, I was wishing that in some areas of my life, I could wipe the slate clean and begin again, eradicating mistakes and sins with their consequences, start afresh. The giants of Regret and Despair were holding me fast. It was rather like *Christian* in John Bunyan's *Pilgrim's Progress,* travelling from the *City of Destruction* to the *Celestial City.* He and his companion *Hopeful,* had gone from the main path, climbed over the stile and strayed unknowingly onto the grounds of *Giant Despair.* He had imprisoned them in *Doubting Castle.* They lay day after day, beaten, starved and full of fear, for the Giant threatened to kill and eat them.

There seemed to be no way out, but suddenly Christian cried out: "O how stupid I have been! I have the key of *Promise* here! It will unlock the dungeon door!" he struggled to his feet and tried the key. It turned, *easily.* The two friends crept through the castle and were going across the courtyard, when Giant Despair caught sight of them and ran to catch them. But suddenly, one of his fits came upon him and he fell down, paralyzed. The key of God's promises had opened the door and overcome despair, suffering and death! They quickly found their way onto the King's Highway again, and set up a notice to warn others not to go on that road.

I saw that regrets and worry were holding me in Doubting Castle. It was time to take the key of Promise and come out of my dungeon.

Outwardly, nothing had changed. The difficult, imprisoning circumstances were still there, but with God's help, I started throwing off the negative ballast of the Past and embracing his plans for my future. Again, I remembered that with God there is always a new beginning, always sunrise after sunset, forgiveness after sin, hope instead of despair. We work together with him to cause these things come to pass in our lives. We might move to a new home, area or job, take a new marriage partner, and seek to *burn our bridges.* Yet if there are unresolved issues, attitudes that have not been put right, the new beginnings become sour and we drink the cup of disappointment.

My willingness and submission would allow the Holy Spirit to move in my heart. Instead of being at cross-purposes, I could begin again, to wait and co-operate with him, and he would do what I could not do! My boat had been too long in the harbour! It was time to pull up the anchor and set my sails to the wind of the Spirit. There was new direction, new vision and new service – **for my God is a God of new beginnings!**

****

Do this, before you run!

'Now when the Philistines heard that they had anointed David king over Israel, all the Philistines went up to search for David. And David heard of it and went down to the stronghold. The Philistines also went and deployed themselves in the Valley of Rephaim. So David inquired of the LORD, saying, "Shall I go up against the Philistines? Will You deliver them into my hand?" And the LORD said to David, "Go up, for I will doubtless deliver the Philistines into your hand." ' II Samuel 5:17+19 NKJV

'Therefore David inquired of the LORD, and He said, "You shall not go up; circle around behind them, and come upon them in front of the mulberry trees. And it shall be when you hear the sound of marching in the tops of the mulberry trees, then you shall advance quickly. For then the Lord will go out before you to strike the camp of the Philistines." ' II Samuel 5:23 + 24 NKJV

David had been king over Judah for two years when the elders of the people came and anointed him king also over Israel. Here we read that when David's old enemies, the Philistines, heard about him being established in his kingdom, they all came and set up their armies to fight him. As soon as David knew this, he asked the Lord if he should go up and fight them. David was a seasoned man of war. He and his "mighty men" had fought many battles and used many strategies to win victories, yet he humbled himself and asked the Lord what he should do. The first time, God gave him the go-ahead, assuring him that he would win the victory, and that is what happened.

When I read this recently, I thought how this often happens in our lives. You have probably heard the phrase: **New levels, new devils!** It is certainly true that when we come to a new level, a new understanding, a new position in God and his Word -- Satan comes to weaken or distract us, to attack in various ways, trying to put us off course, just as the Philistines came when they heard of David and his new position. But David did the right thing – he enquired of the Lord. This is important for us, too. *Lord, how shall I deal with this new attack? Give me your wisdom, show me your divine strategies to stand firm and rout the enemy!*

Then came a second attack from the Philistines; once more, David asks the Lord what he should do. He could have thought: *God told me what to do last time, I'll do that again.* Probably many of us would have done the same, but no, he asked the Lord. Here God changed his tactics. They were not to show themselves to the enemy from the front, but come round behind them, all the time listening for the sound of marching in the tops of the mulberry trees. (*God's marvellous sound-effects, better than any Hollywood can offer!*) When they heard the signal, they should attack full on, for God would be fighting for his people! David informed his captains and mighty men of the new plan, they obeyed, and God caused them to win another great victory!

We might wonder why God did it differently this time. He does not always work the same way in our lives, either. We cannot put him and his ways in a box, thinking *we* have everything under control and know *exactly* how things will turn out. God may have many reasons why he changed the tactic for David, or **he may just have wanted to test David's obedience and humility. I am sure he wants to do that in our lives too, sometimes! So let's "enquire of the Lord", ask his direction and methods instead of running ahead of him, and we will see new victories and be established in a new way in our Christian life!**

****

Eagle Vision or *Spiritual* Vision?!

Passing an optician's shop, I saw a large poster in the window which depicted an eagle and the words:

An eagle doesn't need an eye-test – BUT YOU DO!!

Eagles have a highly developed sense of sight which allows them to easily spot prey. I read they have excellent 20/5 vision compared to an average human who only has 20/20 vision. This means eagles can see things from 20 feet away that we can only see from 5 feet away, allowing them to see clearly about eight times as far as humans can! An eagle is said to be able to spot a rabbit for his dinner 3.2km (2 miles) away!

I smiled at the poster. Yes, it was right, there is no comparison between an eagle and a human's eyes. They certainly did not need a pair of specs!

Having developed cataracts, I had several special eye-tests. First they operated on my left eye, where the old lense was taken out and an artificial one was put in. Before the surgery, I had not been able to see anything at all in that eye for about one year, only light or dark. Afterwards, a new world opened up, crystal clear and with bright colours!

Recently I had surgery on my right eye, and after eight weeks, went to get some new glasses. The old glasses were no longer any good; a procedure had been done and now a **change had come about. I now had different vision.**

The Bible has much to say about "sight" and "vision", physical and spiritual. Jesus healed many people who were blind. Sometimes he touched them, sometimes spoke the Word, one time he spat on the ground, made a muddy paste and spread it on the man's eyes, telling him to go and wash, and he would be healed. In Mark 8:25-26 we read that when Jesus was healing a blind man, the man "looked up. I see men. They look like walking trees. So Jesus laid hands on his eyes again. The man looked hard and realized that he had recovered perfect sight, saw everything in bright, twenty-twenty focus." MSB

2 Corinthians 4:4 tells that the god of this age (Satan) has blinded those who do not believe. Every human-being born on this earth has blind spiritual eyes, blind to spiritual values. But God sent Jesus "..to

open their eyes, and to turn them from darkness to light, and from the power of Satan unto God, that they may receive forgiveness of sins, and inheritance among them which are sanctified by faith that is in me." Acts 26:18

Paul, the Apostle, said to King Agrippa, "I was not disobedient to the vision from heaven", meaning the calling, the vision to carry the Gospel to the Jews and the Gentiles, which Jesus had given him. When we give our life to Jesus and become born-again, our spiritual eyes are opened -- **new vision.** Even like the man who first saw men who looked like trees, then later he could see clearly, that was a progressive healing. As we grow in our Christian walk, there is also a progression. We gain spiritual insight and understanding. God will speak to us too, and give us "callings" and "visions". It may not be a *physical vision,* but God has plans and spiritual visions and inward illumination, to give to us.

One way God increases our inward sight and vision is by the reading of his Word, the Bible. We read the Psalmist prays in Psalm 119:18 --

"Open my eyes, that I may behold wondrous things out of your law." **NLT**

Yes, this Word is full of wonderful things! This is a prayer that God loves to answer. So I would encourage you today to reach out for new vision and let's expect new truths to burst upon our horizon, as our eyes receive new spiritual clarity!

****

Forgive us our Trash-Baskets!

"... and forgive us our trespasses, as we forgive those who trespass against us..." Matthew 6:12 KJV

Little eight-year old Johnny had been learning ***The Lord's Prayer***, in Sunday School. The following week, his teacher looked around at her little class and asked, "Who would like to recite *The Lord's Prayer* for us?" Johnny's hand shot up, "Me, Miss!" "Right – off you go then, Johnny!" All went well... *"Our Father who art in Heaven..."* until Johnny got to *"and forgive us..."* for here, Johnny said with emphasis: "and **forgive us our trash-baskets, as we forgive those who trash basket against us!"**

Teacher tried to explain it was 'trespasses' which means 'sins', but Johnny was sure his version was the correct one, and wouldn't be convinced! I had a good laugh when I heard this, yet in one way, Johnny had hit the nail on the head! We have a good many '*trash-baskets'* in our lives for which we need to ask the Lord's forgiveness, stuff which needs to be got rid of, rotten and nasty. And we also need to forgive the rubbish and hurts which people do against us.

I was thinking of this a few days ago as I watched a neighbour taking apart the wooden decking in his garden. It was in such bad repair, so rotten and falling to pieces that it could not be walked on. It took up almost half of the garden, and something needed to be done about it. So he set to work breaking up all the timbers, and making a big mess. Then there were many trips to take it all to the front drive, where a firm came with a lorry to cart it all away.

The space was then swept and cleared and the neighbour laid down rolls of turf. It had taken a lot of time and hard work, but now the garden looks very neat and tidy; it can be walked on and completely used. It had been well worth the effort! It made me think of the '*trash-baskets'* we need to get rid of in our lives; the broken things we hang onto, perhaps out of habit, stubbornness or we just don't realise how they are hindering us. We may be looking *backwards,* remembering what it was like before, but that chapter is now closed. If we would start to look *forward* and prepare for Tomorrow, we would see what the situation is now. Perhaps we are in a state of denial or refuse to get rid of those 'trashbaskets'?

Or we may feel it is too much trouble to change our thinking, it is easier to go on as we are doing now. If we would have to do everything in our own strength, that might be correct. But we have the **Greater**

One – our Jesus – on our side who will make everything new in our lives, if we will have the courage, obedience and determination to give it into his hands, and let him change us for the better! It won't happen overnight, and as the decking was broken up and looked a terrible mess at first, when we bring our 'trash-baskets' out into the open, things may look worse than they were! But that's when the Holy Spirit takes over, cleansing our hearts, breaking old habits, doing his very special work!

Prayer: Heavenly Father, show us if we have 'trash-baskets' and rotten areas in our lives which need renewing or got rid of. Give us a fresh vision of our hearts as you see them.
Forgive us and help us to pass on this gift of Forgiveness to others, we pray. Holy Spirit, blow your fresh breeze upon us, rejuvenating and quickening us, we ask in the Name of Jesus Christ, our Lord and Saviour. Amen.

****

God is in Control!!

"Do not fear, for I am with you; Do not be dismayed, for I am your God. I will strengthen you and help you; I will uphold you with my righteous right hand," Isaiah 41:10 NIV

It was the morning of my hip surgery and I was wheeled down for the preparations, and the spinal anaesthetic. As they were scrubbing up, I saw the assistant anaesthesist had a lot of tattoos on his arms. Suddenly one stood out; along his forearm were the words -- **GOD IS IN CONTROL!** I pointed to it and said, "I believe that!" He replied, "So do I!"

As he was wheeling me into the Operating Theatre, he told me he had been a Christian for only 18 months. The other tattoos bore witness to a very different lifestyle! He was a shining testimony in a place where people are in need, fear and pain. It seemed like a message from God just for me on that day when I was about to undergo the surgery.

What about you today, my friend? Is everything going marvellously for you or is it difficult for you to see at the moment, that GOD IS IN CONTROL? He, who holds the whole world and universe in his loving hands, constantly seeks to reassure us that your life and mine is in his care and keeping, and he has control over every situation which may confront us!

****

GOD OF THE NEW YEAR!!

"... so that you may know the way by which you must go, *for you have not passed this way before." * Joshua 3:4 NIV

"See, the Sovereign Lord comes with power, and his arm rules for him ... He tends his flock like a shepherd: He gathers the lambs in his arms and carries them close to his heart; he gently leads those that have young." Isaiah 40:10a + 11 NIV

"The Lord replied, My Presence will go with you, and I will give you rest." Exodus 33:14 NIV

We are already a few days into the new year, and we all might approach this new season in different ways. Are you one of those who runs in with both feet, eager to see what the year holds and make history yourself!? Or perhaps you are somewhat fearful, wondering what further bad news and circumstances might be waiting for you round the next bend.

When God told Moses to rescue the Children of Israel from slavery in Egypt, the task seemed overwhelming to him, and he said if God would not go with them, he could not possibly take them to the Promised Land. But God assured him, as the above text tells us, that his *Presence --- he himself --- would* go with Moses and the people, and that this fact would bring Moses rest; his heart could be at peace.

Years later, when Moses had died, God instructed Joshua, their new leader, how they were to cross the river Jordan and take the city of Jericho, the gateway to the Promised Land. Joshua then commanded the priests to take the Ark of the Covenant (which symbolised God's Presence) and to step into the river. Then the people -- keeping a required distance -- would know which way to go. They needed guidance for *"they had never passed that way before."*

We too, have not passed this way before. This year is still a closed book to us, but our God is not just the One who was with us last year, he is also the GOD OF THE NEW YEAR! His Presence will go with us and bring us rest, in good and in difficult times. Nothing takes him by surprise. He has been mapping out our way, putting things in place, pulling 'strings', arranging, sending the Holy Spirit to engineer circumstances, networking us together with people he has ordained.

These verses in Isaiah tell us that God is our Sovereign Lord and he is coming to rule and reign in power. His arm has ultimate strength, yet this same powerful One can also be so tender that he takes the weak young lambs, holding them to his heart in love, and he gently leads those sheep that have young ones. Jesus called himself our Good Shepherd, who laid down his life for his sheep. He is also *our Sovereign Lord,* and will reign in strength and power in *our lives*, yet also show us his tenderness in the times that we are weak or vulnerable. We are also told that a nursing mother may forget her child, but that God our Father will *never* forget his Children, bought with the blood of the Lamb of God, Jesus Christ, his Son!

Several years ago, George and I had entered a new sphere of ministry, and were encountering many difficulties. As we were praying, I saw in the spirit a narrow path leading between great over-hanging mountains and boulders. The path grew darker the more I tried to see what lay ahead. It all looked frightening, dangerous and the rocks precarious, as if they would fall on us, as we walked on that path. But as we continued to pray and bind the forces of the evil one in the Name of Jesus, releasing God's plan and purposes, the darkness began to clear and I saw how the path grew wider, and led into a broad landscape. We had never been that way before, but the Almighty One was not just going *with* us, but going *before*, opening the way, like a strong man with a machete cutting down the undergrowth and branches which hinder those trying to walk through the jungle. He will do the same for *you*, when opposition causes you to fear and would hinder your progress. *He is the God of the New Year, all 365 days of it!*

Nazi Germany's Third Reich had ruled since Hitler took over in 1933, with Germany becoming a fascist totalitarian State, spreading terror across Europe. Great Britain entered the Second World War in September 1939. The nation was gripped with fear and anxiety, waiting for the next sirens to go off, announcing more enemy bombs were to be dropped.

The reigning monarch at that time, King George VI, brought comfort and direction to his subjects, as he quoted some lines from the poem ***"The Gate of the Year"*** in his 1939 Christmas radio broadcast to the British Empire:

"And I said to the man who stood at the gate of the year:

'Give me a light that I may tread safely into the unknown'.
And he replied:
'Go out into the darkness and put your hand into the Hand of God. That shall be to you better than light and safer than a known way'. So I went forth, and finding the Hand of God, trod gladly into the night..."

Minnie Louise Haskins

Prayer:

Thank you Heavenly Father, that your Presence will go with us and give us rest in this new year. You are the Faithful One who keeps your Word to your Children. Whether we are needing a strong arm or a loving, tender one -- you will lead, tend and keep us, as the shepherd does his flock. Hold us steady with the anchor of your Word, when fear would overwhelm, binding its tendrils round us, and send your delivering power to set us free, we pray. We put our hand in your Hand just now, you will bring us safely through and illuminate our path. We ask this in the Name of your Son, Jesus! Amen.

****

Hands off me, you fanatic!!

"When Jesus saw him lie, and knew that he had been now a long time *in that case*, he saith unto him, Wilt thou be made whole?" John 5:6 KJV

"Afterward Jesus findeth him in the temple, and said unto him, Behold, thou art made whole: sin no more, lest a worse thing come unto thee." v.14 KJV

Harold Hill, an ex-NASA scientist and engineer told us how, as a young, eager Christian and having a few healings 'under his belt', he ran to lay hands on an elderly lady in a wheel-chair. But as he started to pray for her, she shouted, *"Take your hands off me, you fanatic! I looked after my husband for over forty years and now it's his turn to look after me! I don't want to get well!"* This was something Harold had not heard of, and he learnt to ask before laying hands on somebody!

In John 5, we see Jesus at the Pool of Bethesda where sick people waited for the "troubling of the waters", and the first one to get in, was healed. Jesus singled one man out who had been ill for 38 years and did not ask him, "Do you want to get well?" but, surprisingly, if he wanted to be made **"whole"**. We might think that if he had not wanted to get well, the man would not be waiting to get in the pool, but *whole?* Jesus healed the man and later on, met him again in the Temple.

Verse 14 shows us that Jesus knew there was a spiritual root to this man's illness, so he warned him not to sin, or something even worse might come, and he would lose his healing. God made us all as a triune being -- body, soul and spirit -- even as he is a Triune Being or Trinity. What we do with our body, the negative things or sins we allow into our mind or spirit can have an outworking in our body, and even bring physical illness. This was the case with the man in John 5. We are not told what his sin had been, but he knew what Jesus was talking about, as he did not question it.

Many sicknesses are purely physical, others we may have brought upon ourselves by our unwise lifestyle. Others have mental or spiritual roots and influences. Another story from Harold illustrates this well. One day, he and some friends were praying for a lady whom the Lord had previously healed of cancer, but now it had returned. They decided to ask if there was a reason for this. The Lord told Harold to ask her if she hated her daughter-in-law. "Yes, I do!" she spat out. "If you will forgive her, God will heal you again," Harold said. *"Forgive her?!! I'd rather die!"* she shrieked, and she did die, soon after.

When I was leading an *Aglow* group in Germany, one of my speakers was a lady who used to be a homeopathic doctor, before becoming a Christian. She had developed cancer and was afraid of what would happen after her death. A friend advised her to go to a Christian weekend retreat, which she did. As she spoke with the counsellor and heard of the Way of Salvation, she was asked to renounce any occult practices she had, knowingly or unknowingly, been involved in. In her practice, she had regularly 'dowsed', using a pendulum and done other occult things, not realising she was opening herself to the powers of darkness. She renounced all this activity and when she got home, she destroyed all her questionable books and closed her practice down.

Not long after, the doctor pronounced her free of cancer. She had received no treatment and the Lord showed her it was because the root of her illness had been her occult involvement. Jesus had made her "whole", spirit, soul and body. [Author's note: While there are a very few Christian homeopathic doctors, and this 'holistic' method or alternative treatment may look very harmless, or just like a method of using herbs rather than chemicals to treat illness, yet this is not the case. Examine who first invented it and the Druid who later introduced it on a wider scale. I am only reporting this case, not suggesting that all people with cancer have participated in any occult practises.]

As you read this today, I do not want you to come under condemnation thinking that you have sinned against the Lord, if you have become sick. But it might be a wise thing to examine our hearts, and ask the Holy Spirit to shine his searchlight into any dark corners. If he finds something and shows us, what we do about it is *our* decision, between us and Jesus. We may need to put some things right, to ask forgiveness, to break off certain friendships or associations which are hindering us, learn to say "No" when stress is sending us into a tail-spin because we are doing a dozen things Jesus never told us to do...

Jesus asks us that question too, *are you, am I* willing to be made *whole*?! If so, there is forgiveness, cleansing and healing waiting for us! Let's reach out for it today!

****

Hey, I'm still here!!

"Is not wisdom found among the aged? Does not long life bring understanding?" Job 12:12 NIV

"Even when I am old and gray, do not forsake me, O God, till I declare your power to the next generation, your might to all who are to come." Psalm 71:18 NIV

"With long life will I satisfy him and show him my salvation." Psalm 91:16 NIV

A friend of mine lost her husband at 60 years old from a terminal illness. I have changed their names and we will call them Wendy and Bob. Having 6 children, they were a close-knit family. Wendy and Bob taught Bible-studies together and took part in many church activities. Bob was also the leader of the local group of an organisation which concentrated on reaching men for Christ, and they organised monthly rallies. Their life was very full and they were an excellent team together.

After Bob's death, Wendy went along to their church workers' meeting, just the same as she and Bob had always done. Various topics were discussed by all, but Wendy was never mentioned and she was given no opportunity to take part in any of the new outreaches. She sat there, not believing her ears and she felt like running out of the room and bursting into tears. But something rose up within her and she said, in a loud, determined voice, **"Hey, I'm still here! Haven't I got anything to give? Can't you use me now that Bob's not here any more?!"**

Everybody was shocked. They had not meant to be unkind, but they had fallen into the old thought that when the husband was no longer there, his widow had to take a back seat, she was not *complete* now that she was on her own. This was not the case, Wendy still had a great deal to give and not long after, she started a Christian group which aimed especially at helping widows spiritually and in practical ways. What the enemy, Satan, had meant for evil, God turned it around for good and used Wendy in a new way.

Some of you who are in England may know the TV program *Hetty Wainthrop Investigates*. Hetty retires from her fulltime job at 60 years old, and realises she may have another 20 or more years ahead of her. What can she fill her time with?! She is already bored on the first day, and she decides to open a private detective agency. With her husband at home taking the phone calls and a teenager who gives her lifts on his moped and undertakes some of the work, she has great success, for who would suspect that this plump, not very fashionably-dressed elderly lady is sizing them up and finding the guilty party?!

Rather like Agatha Christie's *Miss Marple,* who is even older than Hetty, but with a mind as sharp as a tack, who unravels the plot and discovers the murderer!

Well, what has all this got to do with you and me? Simply this, that whatever our age, we can make a difference. God has a place for us, plans to use us for the wellbeing of others and for his glory. While the world — and very often the Church — thinks only of young people being of any use, I believe God thinks differently. People are living longer than they have ever done. Some pastors are recognising this and bringing in a pastor for their elderly congregation who is there especially to help them. Valuable Life-lessons can also be gleaned from elderly people if the younger ones are humble and respectful enough to want to hear from them.

And what about the thinking of us older, or shall I say more *mature* people? Have we grown so set in our ways? Has determination become stubbornness, and we are not prepared to look at any new method, take advice from someone younger, because we think we know it all? If so, let's ask the Lord to change our hearts and thinking, and begin to reach out. Although we may have some physical problems, yet we should also see that *our very life is precious* and it is not just given to us for ourselves, but to influence our world and those we meet, for good. It is easy to withdraw and isolate ourselves, on losing a loved one, either by death, separation or divorce or on going through a tragedy or illness of some kind. Wendy could have done that, but she looked outward and realised that God had a plan for her alone, not just with Bob, and she must discover what that was.

God has promised that he will "satisfy us with long life", that he will carry and care for us until our old age. I want to encourage especially my older readers today, that *you count for something*, God knows just where you are! Shake off despondency and begin to ask the Lord how you can be used by him. He will show us all the next steps to take and open new vistas and doors, bring new

creativity, pour out a new anointing of his Holy Spirit, that we might experience what Psalm 71:18 says --- that we would "show his mighty acts to the next generation!"

****

I HAVE NOT FORGOTTEN YOU!!

"How long, O LORD? Will you forget me forever? How long will you hide your face from me?

How long must I take counsel in my soul and have sorrow in my heart all the day?

How long shall my enemy be exalted over me? But I have trusted in your steadfast love; my heart shall rejoice in your salvation. I will sing to the LORD, because he has dealt bountifully with me." Psalm 13:1, 2+5 ESV

"Can a woman forget her nursing child, that she should have no compassion on the son of her womb? Even these may forget, yet I will not forget you. Behold, I have engraved you on the palms of my hands; your walls are continually before me. " Isaiah 49:15+16 ESV

One morning, my late husband, George, woke up with the following words ringing in his spirit:

"I have not forgotten you!"

He knew the Lord was speaking to him at a time when he was fighting discouragement and depression. What an enormous encouragement it was. Yes, God had *not* forgotten us. He knew all the difficult circumstances we were facing. Unlike ours, his memory never fails. Just as Isaiah the prophet said, our names are engraved on the palms of his hands. When he stretches out an arm, there they are to remind him! *We are not forgotten!*

David the shepherd boy and later king of Israel was mourning over all the difficulties he was facing, and cried to the Lord. He felt God had abandoned him and cast him off, filling his heart with sorrow --- how long would this go on, *forever?!* He saw and heard how his enemies were rejoicing over his downfall. But then he remembered God's goodness and loving-kindness to him in the Past and he broke through into praise. If he had gone according to his feelings, he might not have praised but he made the quality decision which involved his will --"I *will* sing to the Lord".

There are several places in the Bible which tell us that God remembered people.

"The LORD graciously remembered and visited Sarah as He had said, and the LORD did for her as He had promised." Genesis 21:1 AMP

In her old age, the barren Sarah gave birth to Isaac, the son of the Promise.

"Then God remembered Rachel's plight and answered her prayers by enabling her to have children." Genesis 30: 22 NLT

Barren Rachel gave birth to Joseph, whom God used mightily to save multitudes from dying.

Also in 1 Samuel 1:19 we read how God "remembered Hannah" and gave her a son, who would become the prophet Samuel.

When God remembers us, he will turn our barrenness into fruitfulness, our sorrow into joy.

"But God remembered Noah and all the wild animals and the livestock that were with him in the ark." Genesis 8:1 NIV

"And God heard their groaning, and God remembered his covenant with Abraham, with Isaac, and with Jacob." Exodus 2:24 He then provided a deliverer to bring his Covenant people out of slavery.

"You have remembered me, O God," said Daniel, "you have not forsaken those who love you," Daniel 14:38

These are a few examples of God remembering. We may think that if "God remembered", then he must have forgotten these people before. No, that is not the case. It rather means that God's time had come to move on this person's behalf, the conditions had been fulfilled which he had required. We see an example of this in Joseph's life, when shut up unjustly in prison. He interpreted the butler's dream and when he was freed, Joseph asked if he would remember him. But the butler forgot and Joseph had to wait another two years, before Pharaoh had his dreams. Then he said, "I know a Hebrew who can interpret your dreams." Joseph was sent for, and because God gave him the interpretations, Joseph was catapulted from the prison-house to becoming Prime Minister of Egypt, in one day! God had not forgotten his servant! Genesis 40 and 41.

The only thing that God says he will NOT REMEMBER are the sins which we have repented of and confessed to him. This is marvellous news! He says:

"For I will be merciful to their unrighteousness, and their sins and their iniquities will I remember no more." Hebrews 8:12 KJV

Prayer: Heavenly Father, Satan and people would like to tell us that you have forgotten us, that we are not worth bothering about, for we have failed you so often. But your Word tells us that you have not forgotten us. Thank you for your faithful love. We encourage ourselves in you today. You know exactly where we are, all the circumstances we face and you have divine answers, strategies to give us victories. Touch us now with your Holy Spirit, quicken us and fill our hearts with the assurance that we are not forgotten! We praise your wonderful Name! Amen.

****

It's not the End – just a new Beginning!!

"Do not remember the former things, Nor consider the things of old. Behold, I will do a new thing, Now it shall spring forth; Shall you not know it? I will even make a road in the wilderness And rivers in the desert. The beast of the field will honor Me, The jackals and the ostriches, Because I give waters in the wilderness And rivers in the desert, To give drink to My people, My chosen. This people I have formed for Myself; They shall declare My praise." Isaiah 43:18-21 NKJV

"He heals the brokenhearted and binds up their wounds," Psalm 147:3 ESV

Recently was the 20th Anniversary of "Ground Zero" -- when we remember how terrorists flew planes into the World Trade Center, the Twin Towers in New York, USA, killing almost 3000 people and injuring hundreds of thousands. On a Christian TV program, I heard the testimony of a "first responder", a policewoman, who was called to the scene almost immediately after the attack. At that time she was in her 20's and not a born-again Christian.

She described the absolute chaos, huge heaps of rubble and hundreds trying to run away, and the horror of seeing people jumping from skyscraper windows many storeys up, rather than being burnt alive. Covering everything was a huge cloud of dust and ashes, filled with every type of toxin, powdered glass from the numerous plate-glass windows, cancer-causing chemicals, which they were all breathing in. At that time there was no special equipment, breathing apparatus or fireproof clothing for her and her colleagues to wear, just a fireman's helmet with no face shield.

The smell of burning smoke and flesh filling her nostrils remained with her for a long while afterwards. They worked for nearly three months, with very little time off, but few people were 'rescued,' they were 'recovered' -- their bodies or body parts. A few weeks after, this lady started to be ill with all kinds of symptoms, which her doctor could not explain. She became so ill she went to a specialist, who told her she had a "9/11" illness. Thousands of "first-responders" and volunteers were becoming ill, many died in the following months and years following, as a direct result of being exposed to the poisons.

She became a Christian, was baptised in the Holy spirit and got married, but as her condition worsened and she was tortured with the sights and sounds she had witnessed, she felt a physical and emotional wreck. Her oesophagus was full of lesions and she was in constant pain. Her future looked bleak and she was kept alive by a cocktail of drugs. Her husband was very encouraging and supportive, and believed that God would bring her through and heal her. She began to have thoughts of suicide -- that seemed the only way out --- and these became more frequent.

One night when she was in the depths of despair, she turned on a Christian TV program. A man was preaching, suddenly he wheeled round and pointed his finger right into the camera, saying, "You are thinking of taking your own life, of committing suicide! Satan is telling you, you have no future, you might as well end it all! Jesus Christ is your answer and he is saying, It's not the end – it's a new beginning!" This lady knew God had spoken right to her, and something broke free in her life that night. Some of the mental torture left and a new peace came; she began to reach out for God in a new way.

She and her husband went to the church of this preacher, to attend a series of special meetings. Not realising that they were there during the beginning of September, in the meeting held on the 11th, a prophetic word was given about "Ground Zero" in a person's life being healed! She realised that for the very first time, she was no longer bound by the mental and emotional trauma! God had set her free. The couple are now at Bible School, preparing for ministry.

"9/11" was the beginning of the war on terrorism, not only in the USA but around the world. In every war many of those who fought carry mental as well as physical scars for years, perhaps the rest of their life, and many do commit suicide. I knew a man in his 80's who still had nightmares about the hand to hand fighting he had to do in Stalingrad during World War II, 50 years earlier. I was once going to preach in an American church, and the Thursday before, the Lord began to speak to me about some of the men in the congregation who were contemplating suicide, because of what they had experienced and seen on the battle fields of Iran and Afghanistan. Women are more prone to talk about their emotional needs, but men usually hide them and it eats away inside --- whether we are a Christian or not.

On the Sunday morning after I had preached and prayed for a lot of people who had come forward, I shared what the Lord had shown me, giving an invitation for these men. It took courage to do this, but four men in their 40's came for prayer, broken and weeping. That morning God did a lot of deliverance and healing!

I wonder if somebody reading this, is tempted by this lie, that it would be better to end it all. Not only people who have been in terrible situations of destruction and war, but in normal everyday Life, can be tempted in this way. During the pandemic, suicides and attempted suicides have risen; even ministers -- some from mega churches -- have taken their life, and our God of compassion is reaching out his arms to us today to take us in, set us free and heal our brokenness. He wants to make this true for us too ---

It's not the End – just a new Beginning!!

****

JESUS IS THE GREATEST!! by George Jesze

There always were, and always will be people who claim to be "THE GREATEST". At the height of their fame *The Beatles* declared that they were more popular than Jesus! They further said that in a short time Jesus Christ would be completely forgotten and the Bible would hold no more influence today. *The Beatles* made a great mistake, for their pop-group was dissolved and their popularity is just a memory.

Then there was Cassius Clay, the boxer, who declared: "I am the GREATEST!" Later, he was out of the running, a sick man and his victories in the ring were also nothing but a memory. But there is one who was and still is THE GREATEST – **JESUS CHRIST!**

1. HE IS THE GREATEST BECAUSE HE IS THE CREATOR!

In John 1:3 we read: "All things were made by him and without him was not anything made that was made." Although his creation has often forgotten and ignored him, it does not alter the fact that he is the CREATOR.

2. JESUS IS THE GREATEST BECAUSE HE WAS CONCEIVED BY THE HOLY SPIRIT AND BORN OF A VIRGIN.

Many people, even Bishops, disbelieve this fundamental truth of the Christian Faith. If Jesus had been 'fathered' by a man, he would not be the Son of God, or be able to become the Redeemer of Mankind. Jesus must be greater than us because we are only created beings and he is the Creator, far greater than we could ever imagine him to be. He can never be understood by our earthly wisdom.

Why should it be difficult to believe that the Holy Spirit could put the divine Seed of Jesus into Mary's womb? He does the same thing every time a person becomes a Christian. Millions of people throughout the centuries have had the life of Jesus planted in their dead spirits, giving them the NEW BIRTH! We are born "of the Spirit" into the family and Kingdom of God (John 3:5+6).

3. JESUS IS THE GREATEST BY HIS LIFE.

He never sinned, even in word. No fault could be found in him. There was never another life like Jesus' life. He stands far above all the deities of every cult. If he had sinned only once, God would never have accepted his sacrifice for our sin on the cross.

4. JESUS IS THE GREATEST BY HIS CRUCIFIXION!

He gave his life voluntarily, the Good Shepherd who gave his life for the sheep. He was not a martyr who died for a good cause and had no other choice. It was love for us that nailed him to the cross. He died to set us free from the rule and power of Satan and sin. Jesus' life and death were not just an EXAMPLE, he was our SUBSTITUTE. It was as though we were crucified there with him, but *his was the pain and ours is the blessing*! The Son of God who knew no sin became sin for us!

The rocks were torn asunder and Nature revolted, the sun was darkened at this terrifying spectacle. No wonder Jesus cried, "My God, my God, why hast thou forsaken me?!" Paul writes in 2 Corinthians 5:21 "For he has made him to be sin for us, who knew no sin, that we might be made the righteousness of God in him".

Jesus' body was so wounded, beaten and whipped that his back became like a furrowed field. He would probably have received 39 lashes with the scourge. I read that there are 39 main types of diseases – one lash for each of these! "...by whose stripes ye were healed" (1 Peter 2:24 KJV). If Jesus was willing to take this terrible torture on himself, then we should no longer doubt his willingness to heal our body. Redemption includes not only deliverance from and forgiveness for sin, but also healing for our mind and body.

5. JESUS IS THE GREATEST BECAUSE HE ROSE FROM THE DEAD!

When Jesus cried out, "It is finished!", that was not the end of all he was about to do in the act of Redemption. Three days and three nights his body laid in the tomb, but his spirit went and "preached to the spirits in prison" (1 Peter 3:19). Those who believed on him as the Messiah, also rose with him at his resurrection.

Jesus took the prince of captivity – Satan – captive, took back from him the keys of Death and Hell, robbing him of his power, and emerged in triumph! Too long have we allowed the devil to reign over us, quoting verses like Romans 8:28, believing that everything that comes our way must be from God and his Will. We are living in enemy territory, and while some of the trials we experience may be God moulding and shaping us, yet others are a direct attack from Satan. "Resist the devil and he will flee from you..."James 4:7. Why resist if everything is according to the Will of God? May the Lord give us discernment and clarity through his Word in each situation, and wisdom how to handle it. Let's come out of false humility and take our place at Jesus' side, seated in heavenly places (Ephesians 2:6).

6. JESUS IS THE GREATEST BECAUSE HE IS COMING AGAIN!

Only a Jesus who is resurrected, can come again! What a day that will be! We do not know the day or the hour, so let us be ready, and faithfully work and proclaim the message of Salvation, bringing glory to the Name of Jesus! Let us proclaim the WHOLE JESUS to the world – Saviour from sin, Baptiser in the Holy Spirit, Healer and the One who is coming again to take his People home.

SO LET'S PROCLAIM THE MESSAGE OF OUR JESUS WHO IS THE GREATEST --- SO MANY ARE WAITING TO HEAR THIS GOOD NEWS!!

****

Jesus, you have done all things well!

"I have said these things to you, that in me you may have peace. In the world you will have tribulation. But take heart; I have overcome the world." John 16:33 ESV

"Then our mouth was filled with laughter, and our tongue with shouts of joy; then they said among the nations, The Lord has done great things for them. The Lord has done great things for us; we are glad." Psalm 126:2-3 ESV

It was on the afternoon of 11th April 2020, that the Lord took my darling husband, George, home to be with Him. His health had been deteriorating for a good while, and during the last three weeks he had taken a turn for the worse. On the Thursday before Resurrection Sunday, the words came strongly to me: "His feet are on the threshold", so although the doctor had said he might live another week, I knew it would not be that long. There were no special Goodbyes or words to remember, as he was unconscious most of the last week, and with the sun streaming in through the window and the cherry tree in blossom outside, George peacefully breathed his last.

It had been a difficult last three weeks, as I was up and down, night and day, nursing and caring for him. Because of COVID 19, I had carers come to help only right at the end. Some kind friends wanted to come in and lay hands on George, believing the Lord would raise him up, but I knew his time had come. As I now looked at his body on the bed, so thin as he had hardly eaten for three weeks, the words came strongly to me and I spoke them out: **"Jesus, you have done all things well!"**

Yes, although my husband of 54 years was now dead, **Jesus, you have done all things well!** Yes, although I had not expected this: **You have done all things well!!** Your Will is best! Every battle with ill-health, every disappointment that he could no longer be taking much part in Life and that his horizon of activity had become so limited --- that was now all over, and George had seen Him in whom he had believed; he was now vibrant and healthy, basking in the love and wonder of being in Heaven with his Lord. *Jesus, you have done all things well!*

Two weeks later, one of my sons and my daughter-in-law went with me to see George at the Funeral Home. He was dressed in a smart grey suit, white shirt and with his favourite blue tie. In his hands he held the German Bible which he had bought on going to Switzerland as a young minister in 1963. It was open at the 23rd Psalm, one of his favourites. At his feet was his English Bible. I still had other Bibles from him, but these had been his 'tools of trade', used in countless sermons in different countries, through the years. *They belonged to him, even now,* I thought!

As we were there and I looked at his body in the coffin, again the words sang in my heart: ***Jesus, you have done all things well!*** This was only the 'shell' which had housed his spirit, *George was long gone!* A few days later was the funeral. I was feeling quite weak and trembly as I had hardly slept or eaten for three weeks, so we took a folding chair for me to sit on during the graveside service. I just stood up for the internment and as we sang "Blessed assurance, Jesus is mine". Then as the bearers lowered George's coffin into the grave, again the words resounded in my spirit: ***"Jesus, you have done all things well!"*** They were not just words, I believed them and I still do now!

In every one of our lives there are situations we did not expect, would not choose and which we would do anything to avoid; paths that God leads us on which we cannot understand, which we may fight against, where we struggle to know whatever is happening. This may not be the death of a loved one, we can think of many other examples. I have had many other situations apart from George's passing (and still have), where I have had to choose to say that Jesus has done all things well.

I want to encourage you today, if you are going through one of those times right now, that this holds true also in *your life* – your Heavenly Father has all things in his hand, -- *let go and let God* **work out his purposes for and in you. He still has a Resurrection Morn for you after the death of your hopes! May the day come soon when you will be able to say with all your heart:**

Jesus, you have done all things well!

****

Joy and Challenge of Summer Days

"God saw all that he had made, and it was very good." Genesis 1:31a NIV

It hadn't been there when I came before in April. I looked with delight at the candy-striped geraniums, the mass of flowers interspaced with natural white stones, neatly protected by a criss-cross wooden fence – a splash of colour in the old flagged yard, surrounded on three sides by shabby houses and on the other, the Gypsy church. Once again I was amazed at the power of the Gospel of Jesus Christ which can transform wife-beaters and drunkards – as so many of the Gypsies or 'travellers' had been – into people who were learning to live a new life, to build up and make a home, instead of living in squalor and chaos, to become creative, take pride in what they do and make the church yard beautiful, for this was *God's* House!

This had been in Debrecen, Hungary, where I was with a group of leaders and pastors from East and West at a meeting hosted by a charity which works in Europe. After two intense days of planning and sharing, there was the wild dash of three hours to the Budapest airport in broiling heat, hanging on as the driver dodged accidents, road-works and traffic-jams, to the despair of the driver in the car following! Back at the Dutch office near Rotterdam, we stayed in the apartment above the office, working on UK and international administration.

It had all been very satisfying but tiring, and after preaching in a Nigerian church in The Hague on Sunday, we were glad to relax with a choc ice in front of the TV. Suddenly we were transported to England, again to a garden, but this time to some *magnificent* ones, for the program *Songs of Praise* was just on, coming that Sunday from a Castle Garden in Kent.

The large choir standing on the lawn brought us joy with their marvellous singing, while through the eye of the camera we wandered from a wave of bluebells under the trees, to beds of blue delphiniums and scabius, the reds, yellows and orange of the cottage garden and where ox-eyed daisies waved in tall grass. There were glimpses of a stone cat and a statue peeping through foliage, a grey tower majestic in the distance cameoed by box hedges; purple clematis dripped down the sides of the mellow old house, while the clean lines of the severely cut hedges had a beauty of their own.

A lady told how she had opened her substantial garden to the public, inviting individuals or small groups to the garden for a time of peace and tranquility, to meditate and find themseves again, to take stock in the headlong rush of busy, modern life. Lines from a time-honoured poem were quoted:

"You're nearer God's heart in a garden
    Than anywhere else on earth..."

Of course, we know the very first person to plant a garden was God himself (Genesis 2:8), and it does seem that healing and wholeness steal into our hearts as we wander round or sit in a wellkept garden.

It's high Summer and this is the time when flowers burst forth but also the *weeds,* and they have to be dealt with! Our lives too, are filled with the contrasts of beauty and quietness on the one hand, and the challenge and hectic demands of our schedule on the other. Jesus said to his disciples that they should come apart and rest awhile, for sometimes they did not even have time to eat. The crowds were so eager to see and hear him, so desperate to receive healing that they thronged him, sometimes for days on end.

It is a trap we can easily fall into -- I have done it too -- that when ministering to people and seeing the enormous needs, we overstretch ourselves, becoming "burnt out" or having a nervous breakdown, trying to help. We need to find the balance of work and play, ministry and relaxation, learning when to say "Yes" or "No" if asked to take on yet another task, asking the Lord for his guidance about it first.

So dear Friends, I wish you another wonderful Summer week, on holiday or at home, sometimes sitting in your garden or off to ministry taking Christian Summer Camps, perhaps going on missionary journeys to preach or take relief goods to those in need abroad. As we experience **the joy and challenge of Summer days**, let's hold fast to our Jesus, who is with us in the good times and also there when it seems as though the rug has been pulled out from under our feet – he will uphold us with his strong right arm, and bring us through every storm! I pray strength for every task and peace to you, from Jesus, our great Prince of Peace!

****

JOY BECAUSE JESUS CAME!!

"... she (Mary) gave birth to her firstborn, a son. She wrapped him in cloths and laid him in a manger, because there was no room for them in the inn." Luke 2:7 NIV

"For to us a child is born, to us a son is given; and the government shall be upon his shoulder, and his name shall be called Wonderful Counselor, Mighty God, Everlasting Father, Prince of Peace." Isaiah 9:6 ESV

The other day I was thinking about the Christmases I enjoyed as a child, growing up in the South of England. There was no money for a Christmas tree, but homemade decorations, red-berried holly stuck behind the pictures, a sprig of mistletoe hanging from the lamp gave it all a festive air. The Sunday School party had come and gone with games and the two poor little brothers who had stolen some cakes and slid them down into an umbrella to take home! But nobody said anything, for we knew they did not have much food.

My parents, not wanting to rob me of all the fun, yet not wanting to tell lies, used an original name for a certain red-coated, white-bearded gentleman. I remember when I was four years old, my father bent down and called up the chimney: "Father at Christmas, Helen's been a naughty girl this year, perhaps you don't want to bring her any presents!" My fears were groundless, however, for "Father at Christmas" did bring in a pillow-slip filled with knobby bundles, which I found at the end of my bed on Christmas morning. My presents were usually jigsaw puzzles, handkerchiefs, a tiny bottle of "Evening in Paris" perfume and the inevitable books, for I loved to read.

On the radio we listened to the Queen's speech, and then heard the well-known entertainer (was it Wilfred Pickles and his wife, Mabel?) go round the wards of a well-known children's hospital, as he talked with sick children and gave them presents. On Boxing Day (26th December in England) after lunch the guests would start to arrive. They were friends from the church my father pastored. Coats were piled on the bed; a hot cup of tea and one of Mum's mince-pies and a seat by the bright coal fire gave a welcome.

When all had arrived the games would start. "Pass the Parcel" and

"Charades" were firm favourites, while Mr. P., an ex-Scout Master, always had plenty of games, jokes and riddles to keep us going. Later on, the table was laid with the china "Cottage Garden" tea service, and we all tucked in to sandwiches, jellies, sausage-rolls, mince-pies and Mum's iced Christmas cake. Then there were carols round the piano, for didn't we only have Christmas because Jesus came to Earth to die for us...?

It was all simple fun and fellowship, but I love to remember those times. Nowadays, materialism has hidden the true meaning of Christmas, while political correctness even wants to rob us of our right to celebrate his birth at all! Many Christmases have come and gone since then, and this time of Advent points us to the next Christmas, which will soon be upon us. Advent also reminds us that one day, not too very long, Jesus will come again to catch away his born-again children. This time he will not come as a helpless, vulnerable baby, but as the victorious King of Kings!

Here's wishing you and your family much joy this Christmas ---
BECAUSE HE CAME!

****

NEW BEGINNINGS!

"As far as the east is from the west, so far hath he removed our transgressions from us." Psalm 103:12 KJV

"He shall again have compassion on us; He will subdue *and* tread underfoot our wickedness [destroying sin's power]. Yes, You will cast all our sins into the depths of the sea." Micah 7:19 Amplified Bible

"Return, O backsliding children," says the LORD; "for I am married to you... Jeremiah 3:14a NKJV

Every new year has a new beginning, a new season. In daily life, some things go on the same as the year before, but others change and even come to an end. God is always a God of new beginnings, a new day -- not just one of 24 hours -- but a new chapter, a God of sunrise and not sunset. Some things we take gladly into the new year, but others, it would be better if we left them behind us. Are you one of those who makes New Year Resolutions? Recently I heard a group of people tell of theirs, several resolving to give up chocolate!! Might be a good idea for some of us!

But going deeper than that, I am thinking of experiences from the Past which we have dragged into every new year and these are hindering us. Satan accuses us, pointing out our flaws, our sins, and we become so discouraged. Outwardly it might look as though we have it all together, but inwardly, we are becoming hopeless and feel God can't possibly forgive us again. George used to say that when we make a mistake, the devil comes and takes a photo of it. Soon he has a whole gallery, and when we come to the Lord for something, he gleefully shows us all our mistakes, to weaken and discourage us.

I read about a pastor in Africa who had fallen into sin, and was backslidden for a while. Later he came back to the Lord and was very ashamed. He felt as though his family, life and ministry were over -- that he was just a failure. In despair he cried out to God, and in the night he had a dream. An angel came to him with a big book in his hand, and showed the pastor pages from the book, then read out what was written there. "On that date you did this for the Lord; here you helped that person ..."

It sounded all very positive, yet as they got nearer to the date of his downfall, the pastor got more and more nervous. To his surprise, that page was blank and several pages after it. "What happened here?" he asked. The angel replied, "On the other pages *you* were working for *God*, that's what *you* did, but on these *blank* pages this is what *he* did for *you!*" The pastor was set free! His burden of guilt dropped off of him, as he realised God had not left him! All the time he was working by his Spirit to bring his child back! This pastor had a new revelation of God's mercy and grace. His family and ministry were restored.

Our Scripture verses here assure us of God's love and forgiveness for us also, when we fall back into our old lifestyle, not living as close as we should to Jesus, or perhaps even wandering very far away. Perhaps this has happened to you, and you want to come back, but you are not sure whether you will be welcome again in the Father's Family, that your Christian life is a failure and your ministry a thing of the Past.

Let me encourage and urge you today, to realise *God* has been working *for you* on the 'blank pages' of your life. "The goodness of God leads us to repentance!" Throw yourself on his mercy today, experience the cleansing and deliverance of the blood of Jesus, receive a fresh revelation of this merciful God!

But it is also good to ask the Holy Spirit if there were definite reasons why we have backslidden or fallen into sin. He may reveal things where we have left a spiritual or mental door open, and Satan has had here the advantage – the 'walls of our city' were broken down. Let us learn from the past, let God use it to change us for the better, to give us more understanding for others who have gone this way, and perhaps we have criticised them in our hearts; here too, we are told that when we think we are standing, we should take heed lest we fall. Our self-righteousness is as filthy rags in God's sight – it is in his strength alone that we stand!

Prayer: Heavenly Father, thank you for restoring this dear pastor and so many others, us too, when we have turned away from you. Let this year be a NEW BEGINNING where we turn from our failures, and accept your forgiveness, walking in newness of Life with you! Thank you for a fresh revelation of your mercy and your grace, we pray, and help us to show your compassion to those around us, restoring the broken and the lost ones. We ask this in the Name of your Son, Jesus Christ, Amen.

****

No Black in Heaven!

"You turned my wailing into dancing; you removed my sackcloth and clothed me with joy," Psalm 30:11 NIV

"Thou hast turned for me my mourning into dancing; thou hast put off my sackcloth, and girded me with gladness; To the end that my glory may sing praise to thee, and not be silent..."Psalm 30:11+12a KJV

This morning I tied the silky scarf loosely round my neck, with its cascade of bright but tasteful colours -- violet, lilac, blue, jade green, black and white. As always when I look at this scarf, I rejoice again that I am able to see and recognise colour – this wonderful, uplifting blessing God has given us. Suddenly I remembered the situation when we had not been living and ministering in Germany very long, how women used to go into mourning and wear black when a family member died. It lasted some months, even up to a year, before they could put away these certain clothes. Furthermore, if someone else in the family died, they would have to go into mourning again. It was noticeable that *men* were not required to do this, only *women*. I was glad I did not have to do this!

Sometimes women came to me for counselling, and it turned out that their depression and heavy burden of oppression was brought on every time they opened that *certain* drawer. The sight of these clothes brought back painful memories and they relived each death again. Women, whom God has made to respond to colour, design, beauty, sensitivity, creativity -- these were the very ones whom tradition --- even the traditions of some church denominations -- required to clothe themselves with garments of mourning; some countries required that even their underwear must be black.

It was clear that this was another ploy of Satan, to trap and enslave women, and they needed to look closely at this and recognise it for what it was, and make the decision not to give him the chance to bind them in this way. I knew a pastor's wife who committed suicide, and another who was about to throw her children down the stairs and then kill herself, too. But Jesus stepped in and prevented this. He showed her the door she had left open, spiritually and mentally, which had given depression free rein with her thoughts. I am not inferring that in these cases the depression came from wearing mourning clothes, but just showing that even born-again Christian men and women can be tormented with this, and Jesus wants to set us free, and hinder it from developing in the first place.

My husband, George, died in April 2020. Although I grieve for him, I do not wear black, but wear normal clothes and colours. If a woman decides to wear black, either in mourning or just anyway, black can look very elegant and not be depressing if teamed with the right colours or accessories, but that is a different matter, and her *choice*, not something she is being forced into.

A late friend of ours, Yorrie, a fiery Welsh preacher and singer, drifted in and out of consciousness a few days before he died. Elaine, his daughter, told me how that one time when he came back and was able to speak to her, Yorrie was describing what he had seen in heaven. He said: **"Oohh! The colours! The colours! There is no black in Heaven, 'Lainey!"** I have heard testimonies of Christians who died and were brought back to life by Jesus, that there were amazing flowers of vibrant colours in Heaven, colours they could not describe because they were not like ones we have here on Earth. It was Yorrie's wish that people should wear Hawaiian shirts at his funeral, and give praise to God for all he had done! He was also buried in his own Hawaiian shirt, and at the funeral, the guests already had their dress code given them! Now that was Yorrie's and the family's choice; I'm not recommending this should be at every funeral!

Satan seeks to oppress men and women, boys and girls in various ways and cause them to wear 'sackcloth' or clothes of mourning. Jesus said that this happened because he is the destroyer, a killer. But he, JESUS, came that we might have LIFE abundantly! Sometimes we have grown so used to our spiritual and mental mourning clothes that we no longer realise how bound we are. It's time to throw them off, and put on the Garment of Praise for the spirit of heaviness, and dance in the Presence of our Mighty Glorious Lord, bringing freedom to ourselves and glory to his Name!

****

On Wings like Eagles!!

"...But they that wait upon the Lord shall renew their strength; they shall mount up with wings as eagles; they shall run, and not be weary; and they shall walk, and not faint." Isaiah 40:31 KJV

I love this Bible verse! It is so full of hope and promise; of assurance that God knows we often feel weak or vulnerable, needing new strength. It is good to look at this verse in context. When we read from verse 28 in the NIV it goes like this:

"Do you not know? Have you not heard? The LORD is the everlasting God, the Creator of the ends of the earth. He will not grow tired or weary, and his understanding no one can fathom. He gives strength to the weary and increases the power of the weak. Even youths grow tired and weary, and young men stumble and fall; but those who hope in the LORD will renew their strength. They will soar on wings like eagles; they will run and not grow weary, they will walk and not be faint."

First God asks if we haven't heard or known that he is the Lord of all the earth, the Creator. He goes on to give us a picture of his greatness and his power, and says he, himself, never grows weary or tired; even young men, who are usually full of life and vigour, can grow weary, stumble and fall, but God does not even know the meaning of the word! He shows us he is the answer.

While the KJV says in verse 31, that those who "wait upon" the Lord will have their strength renewed, the NIV says those who "hope in the Lord". Another translation says: those who "trust in the Lord". If we "wait upon" the Lord, then we will be hoping and trusting him for the answers. Spending time in prayer, in reading his Word, in worship and praise, enjoying his presence are all ways we can have our strength renewed. Sometimes I lay on my bed, listening to a CD or cassette tape (yes, I still have some!!) with worship music on, or someone reading from the Bible and let that sink into my spirit and my soul, gathering strength for my day.

God promises that we will run and not grow weary, walk and not faint, and that we will even "soar like an eagle" (NIV), and it's that I would like to unpack a little here. The KJV states "mount up" like an eagle. Eagles have wing-spans of 6 to 7.5 feet, some even bigger. They soar high in the sky, but do not 'fly' as most birds. The eagle soars but instead of flapping its wings, it waits on a rock for the thermal winds, till an appropriate air-current comes, then he lets himself be carried high, balancing and adjusting his wings perfectly in the rush of air.

The eagle loves the storm and whereas other birds run for cover, he gives an exultant scream and lets the storm-winds carry him to even greater heights. The wind of the Holy Spirit wants to carry us to a higher level and take the strain and effort out of our Christian life, when we follow his leading. Just like the eagle adjusts to the air current, we must learn to adjust and be adaptable so that we will not be swept off our feet by the wind of problems and new situations.

When somebody climbs a ladder or goes up steps, they go up gradually to reach a new height. But when a person gets on a horse, we call it *"mounting the horse"*. In one go, the person reaches a higher level than the ground on which he was standing before. God is saying that we can soar but also *"mount"* up like the eagle, meaning that he will cause us to gain new spiritual revelation and come to new places in God, by the higher level to which he brings us. The eagle is able to fly so high and does not flap its wings but mounts the air-currents, because it has cylindrical bones and a built-in air-borne capacity. Job 39:27 also states the eagle "mounts" or "climbs" rather than flies.

King Solomon said in Proverbs that one thing he could not understand was "the way of an eagle in the air". This is a picture of the Christian, who, without visible support and human help, acting like God, living from supernatural sources, doing what other people cannot do, lives his life in this world. This is not possible in our own strength and ability, but only by God's power in us.

The eagle uses its wings for another important reason, and that is to show its babies how big and strong they are. The mother eagle does this just when it is time to teach them to fly. She pecks all the soft moss, lamb's wool and feathers out of the nest until the babies are sitting on the bare thorny branches. She lifts one eaglet onto the cliff, and stretches out her huge wings, hovering in front of him, then she tips him over the cliff and he is falling, falling ... But before he smashes onto the rocks below, Mother Eagle swoops down, catches him on those wings and takes him up to the top again. She repeats this until he realises he too, has got some things at the side – not as big as Mum's – and begins to stretch them out, and *he learns to fly.*

This is like us when God shows us he is more interested in our *character* than our *comfort,* and says it is time we left the bottle and nappy stage, so he takes away some of our securities. When we are young Christians God shows us how mighty and wonderful he is. He spreads out his wings of power and answered prayer and we are thrilled. Then comes the time when he pushes us 'over our cliff '. We are sure he is going to finish us off, that there is no way out, then at the last moment he scoops us up, coming to our aid. He does this often, for he is teaching us to spiritually fly!

I once heard a song about eagle Christians. The chorus went like this:

Rise and soar into the sunlight rays
Using both your wings of prayer and praise.
Mount like eagles, higher in the sky,
And you'll find things look so different when you fly!

So, I'd like to encourage you today to wait upon the Lord, find fresh strength and life in him, and mount up on *your wings of prayer and praise.* If you are in a storm at present, let God show you how he can use it to bring you even higher in him, just as the eagle 'mounts' on the storm-wind.

We too, surely will find that things look so different *when we fly!*

****

Practising Pagan or a "New-Lifer"?!

"But you will receive power when the Holy Spirit has come upon you, ... you will be my witnesses in Jerusalem ... Judea and Samaria, and to the end of the earth." Acts 1:8 ESV

Sometimes, as Christians, we find it difficult to talk to other people about Jesus -- to evangelise. One way that helps me, is by ordering a number of the Christian paper *New Life,* and giving them to people who come to the house or that I meet, as the Lord guides me. A few weeks ago I had a hospital appointment with a physiotherapist. When I was finished, I took a *New Life* out of my bag and offered it to her, saying, "I have something here for you, a Christian newspaper, where people tell what God has done in their lives."

Tucking it into my bag again, she said, "I'm a practising pagan, I'm not interested." As I went out, I said with a smile, "Thank you for your honesty, *but if you're not interested in him, God is still interested in you!"*

But usually I have positive reactions. Recently a young man brought a delivery to my house, and before he went, I said, "Just a minute, I have something for you," and handed a *N.L.* to him. "Do you know this Christian newspaper, where people tell how they have found Jesus as their Saviour?" He looked at it with interest and said, "Oh, I'll read this. Are you a Christian? My parents are, but I have not been going to church for a while." "What country do you come from?" I asked, and he named an African country. We went on to have a short but lively conversation, and I sensed that his heart was opening to the Lord, so I said, "I won't keep you long, but may I pray for you?" He looked up with a big smile, then reverently taking off his cap, said, "Yes, please!" The Holy Spirit was working as we prayed together at the door-step. He brought me a delivery and I was able to deliver him something too!

Last week, in a large supermarket, I chose some pots of Spring flowers. When I put my basket on the counter to pay, the shop assisistant took out the first pot with its bright colours and exclaimed, "Aren't they beautiful?! They make you think of *new life!*" "Yes, you're right!" I said and then went on, *"Would you like a new life?"* He looked at me questioningly, as though to say, what do you mean - -- *a new life?!* I laughed and handed him my last *N.L.*, saying, "Here, this *New Life* can tell you how to find a new life in Jesus!" "Well, what a coincidence, you having this paper when I said that!" the man looked astonished. "Could be," I replied, "but I think God arranged that I bring it with me today. It's my last one, *just for you!"* He shook his head, this was a new thought, and he said he would certainly read it.

When carers used to come to my husband, I would often give them a *N.L.* and it opened the way for some very interesting conversations. One of them asked, "Have you got any more of those papers? I read the one you gave me and it was very interesting." "Yes, the new ones have come for this month, here you are!" I replied. "Oh good, I'll read it in my lunch-hour," and off she went.

At Christmas or Easter time I often ordered enough papers for the whole of my street, plus some extra copies to give to people personally. Rolled up neatly with shiny coloured ribbon, and the words written in the margin: "From George and Helen at number 16, Happy Christmas", they were popped through each letter-box with a prayer for the Holy Spirit to use it to bless the readers and cause them to turn to Jesus. We only knew a few families on our street, but this paper would make an introduction.

Something very simple, but a paper or an attractive Gospel tract can often do the work, say the words which we might find difficult, be a conversation-starter. I would encourage you to try it if you haven't already!

Prayer: Heavenly Father, give us creative, God-inspired ideas how to reach others with your Word, how to tell them of your goodness and Plan of Salvation. In these turbulent days, and when people are not knowing which way to turn, shine your love out of our smile, our handshake. Warm numb deadened hearts to Life again, save and deliver, let backsliders be restored, and use us for your glory. In Jesus precious Name, we ask it, Amen.

****

Purchased with the Blood of Christ!

"For you know that it was not with perishable things such as silver or gold that you were redeemed from the empty way of life handed down to you from your forefathers, but with the precious blood of Christ, a lamb without blemish or defect." 1 Peter:18+19 NIV

Once we stayed in a Christian guesthouse in Germany. In the chapel over the altar, hung a banner. It depicted a red cross on a white background, with large drops of blood falling down, and the words: "FULLY PAID!" My heart rejoiced at this proclamation, that with his blood, my Saviour had paid the price for my sin, and that of the whole world, if they would only accept it.

Nowadays, we do not hear many sermons about the blood of Jesus, nor is it mentioned too often from the pulpit. Many Christians want a *"bloodless"* Christianity. Blood is not something we wish to think about. However, the *blood of Jesus is different.* The sinless blood of Jesus Christ, shed on the cross of Calvary bought me free from Satan's bondage!

Growing up in a Christian home and giving my life to Jesus at the age of nine, I had heard a lot about the sacrifice of Jesus, but nobody could talk about Calvary like Bro. Fisher. He was an English missionary who had spent several years in China before the Communist takeover. He and his wife had suffered greatly. One day she died, and not long after, his little daughter, too. The Chinese laughed at his grief and would not make him any coffins. "Throw them from the mountain-side! Let the wolves and the birds get them! *They're only women!"* they scoffed.

So Bro. Fisher cut down some trees and with his own hands made a tiny coffin for his baby and a bigger one for his wife, then all alone, he buried his loved ones. His sorrow pressed him closer into God and Calvary became more real than ever. Yet Calvary was not only sorrow. It is joy and victory, and since then, I have learned this, too. *Afterwards came the resurrection!*

A group of forty people had come to the guesthouse for one of their regular retreats. Each one had been addicted to alcohol, drugs, sex, gambling or some other bondage. Very often, when asked who they were, they would reply something like this: "I am Mr. So-and-So, a drug-addict." They would still say this although they had not taken any drugs for months or years. They still saw themselves in this way. The group-leaders were born-again Christians and God was using them to help these people in need. Some of them had already found Jesus, but most were there for the fellowship, friendship and a few days away, but not yet seeing the need or wanting to reach out to their only hope -- the saving, delivering power of Jesus Christ.

They held their sessions in the chapel, but someone had turned the banner round! It was more popular to continuously talk about one's problems in this self-help group, than to acknowledge the One who had paid for all their sin. But who's talking about 'sin' ? We don't have *sin,* we have a *problem!* Or do we...?

We were saddened to hear it was one of the leaders who had turned the banner round, and prayed that God would give them the courage to impart the truth with great compassion and wisdom, yet uncompromisingly, to those in such desperate need.

Yes, more precious than gold or silver, *the precious blood of Christ!*

****

Peter, feed my Lambs and Sheep!

"The Lord turned and looked upon Peter. And Peter remembered the word of the Lord, how he had said unto him, "Before the cock crow, thou shalt deny me thrice." Luke 22:61 KJV

Jesus turned and looked at Peter, Peter heard the cock outside.
His look said, I still love you, Peter, even though you've me denied.
Peter rushed and blindly groping for the latch upon the door,
Shutting out the crowded courtyard, could not bear it anymore.
Rushing, tripping through the alleys, remorse and anguish welling up,
He had denied his Lord and Master, he had filled his bitter cup.

+++++++

Peter sadly going fishing, hears a voice call from the shore.
Disappointed, has caught nothing: I'm not fishing anymore.
Cast your net out on the right side – did it and then they did take
A multitude of glist'ning fishes and in the net not a single break!
John, he whispered: It is Jesus! Peter looked and jumped right in, Forgot the fishes, only knowing that he right to his Lord must swim.

Jesus, calling from the lakeside: I have food here, come and eat.
Peter, with fried fish and bread, sitting there at Jesus' feet.
No-one dares to ask: Who are you? For they know it is the Lord,
Caring for tired, hungry fishermen, He – the Resurrected Word!
Jesus turned and looked at Peter, in His eyes forgiveness deep.
Peter, if you truly love me, Peter, feed my lambs and sheep!

+++++

Jesus has been taken prisoner. Peter, following to see what would happen to him, warming his hands at the fire in the courtyard with the scoffers and the servants of the High Priest, now denies for the third time that he knows Jesus, and the rooster crows outside. At that very moment Jesus is led out and turns to look at Peter, sorrowfully and searchingly. Then Peter realises that is what Jesus had told him would happen. He rushes away to find a place to weep and the Bible tells us he "wept bitterly".

Simon, the reed which was blown every way in the wind, was being fashioned in the hand of God into "Peter, the rock, or the stone which came out of the big rock". He, who had said he would die for Jesus, had to first plumb the depths of self-discovery, and learn how weak he really was apart from the power of Jesus. Peter denied Jesus and Judas betrayed him. Yet Peter repented and Judas went and hung himself.

Jesus, risen from the dead, shows himself to his disciples, to over 500 people at the same time, to the two disciples walking to Emmaus and to Peter, a special visitation, just for him (Luke 24:34). I wonder what they talked about, but I'm sure Jesus assured Peter of his forgiveness and mercy. In that time of self-discovery, Jesus was with him all the way. Peter's repentance was deep and complete. Every man and woman of God goes through various "wilderness times", where God shapes and moulds us, like the potter making a vessel on the wheel. These come as God plans them, not just because we have sinned or denied Jesus like Peter.

Even though they now knew Jesus had risen from the dead, they did not know what to do next. Jesus, being no longer with them physically had left a great void. So Peter decides to go fishing; some others join him. They toiled all night and caught nothing, then a voice calls from the shore. As they obey his instructions, their boats are nearly dragged under from the weight of so many fishes! Peter, jumps into the sea and swims to that figure – *it must be Jesus,* only *he* could work a miracle like that!

A fire has been made, fried fish and bread are prepared for them all. In wonderment they eat and look at the beloved face of their Lord. Then Jesus again singles out Simon Peter and asks him three times if he loves him. Peter is hurt by this but humbly he says: Lord, you know all things. You know that I love you! Peter then receives a special commission from Jesus: "Peter, feed my lambs and sheep!" He goes on to tell what death he would die to glorify Jesus, but until that time, Peter was to become a mighty Apostle (John 21:3-17).

I wonder if you are feeling you have denied Jesus in some way, and Satan is tormenting you that you cannot be forgiven. The promise is also to you and me:

"But if we walk in the light, as he is in the light, we have fellowship with one another, and the blood of Jesus, his Son, purifies us from

all sin." 1 John 1:7 NIV

This is written to Believers, reminding us that while we walk in the light of God's Word, as he is in the light, we have fellowship with each other, and if we sin but repent, Jesus' blood purifies us from every sin. At our New Birth, the root of sin was taken out of our heart, our spirit, and Jesus planted new life, a new nature, in its place. But this does not mean that we never sin again. However, if we do sin and truly repent, we will be cleansed and forgiven, just as Peter was. So I want to encourage you today, that whatever Satan is tormenting you with, you can stand on that verse and receive cleansing and peace of mind again – **today!**

****

Prepare me a lodging!!

"But withal prepare me also a lodging: for I trust that through your prayers I shall be given unto you." Philemon 22 KJV

This verse came in my Bible reading this morning, and I was reminded about an incident several years ago. George had invited Evangelist Johan Maasbach from The Hague, Netherlands to come and hold a series of meetings in our area, in South Germany, and George would interpret into German. On the morning of the first meeting, in my Bible reading, this same verse stood out to me. I thought it was strange, as the hotel lodgings and everything else was already arranged. Nevertheless, in obedience to the Holy Spirit, I made up five more beds in our house, bought extra food and off we went to the service.

Afterwards, a lady came up and said, "I wonder if you can help me. Four friends and I -- and our dog! --- have come down from North Germany for the meetings and we have nowhere to stay the night, and no money for a hotel." I laughed and said, "The Lord has it all arranged! He spoke to me this morning and I have 5 beds waiting and you are very welcome -- *and the dog!*" In faith they came that God would provide for them, longing to see the Lord at work through Bro. Maasbach. They were not disappointed on either score, for the Holy Spirit worked mightily in the service and a lodging was already prepared!

In 1970, George, I and our 3 year old son were travelling for 7 months, holding meetings in various European countries. We had just reached Northern Germany and a meeting had been cancelled, so we were left with no lodgings and no money for a hotel. There were two more days before we were due at our next place. Our sandwiches were all eaten, and we were almost down to our last German Mark. This was before mobile phones so at the next phone-box, George got out and rang a lady's number which we had been given, in case we were stuck or needed help.

This Christian lady invited us to her house. As we went in, she said, "Now I know about the roast duck!" We were very puzzled as we had no idea what she was talking about. She told us that the Lord had instructed her to buy a duck, and it was already roasting nicely in the oven! She had bought the bird although she could not understand the reason, and living on her own, wondered how she would be able to eat it! Then we unexpectedly turned up! God had gone before, and let me tell you, that duck tasted delicious!! We did not have to go hungry and a most comfortable lodging had been prepared!

When the Apostle Paul wrote those words, he was imprisoned in Rome. Being a Roman citizen, he did not have to stay in prison, but was able to live in his own rented house, chained to a guard. Yet Philemon and many others were praying for his release, so Paul asked that a lodging should be prepared for him as he believed that God would graciously answer.

This year, we have seen many photos showing weary refugees from Ukraine who are fleeing the war but do not yet have the blessing of a lodging. Sometimes they just drop down on the ground to sleep. People in several countries are offering refugees lodgings and practical help. A charity with whom I am associated has just sent off a bus to bring back Ukrainian refugees to Holland. This is a much bigger need than the lodgings that the friends and their dog, or that my little family needed, yet God is concerned about the practicalities of Life, as he sees our broken world, and wants us to come with our big and small needs to him.

Prayer: Heavenly Father, thank you for your loving kindness and the preparations you make for your children and those in need. Show us what you would have us do each day; may we be obedient to your prompting, and give us the strength to undertake the task you put before us. It may be "preparing a lodging" or something quite different to help the needy and to bring glory to you! We pray in Jesus Name, Amen.

****

Holocaust Survivor Rose Price

Remembering God's Chosen People!!

"For you are a people holy to the Lord your God. Out of all the peoples who are on the face of the earth, the Lord has chosen you to be his treasured possession." Deuteronomy 14:2 NIV

"And who is like your people Israel – the one nation on earth that God went out to redeem as a people for himself, and to make a name for himself, and perform great and awesome wonders by driving out nations and their gods from before your people, whom you redeemed from Egypt? You have established your people Israel as your very own forever, and you, O Lord, have become their God." 2 Samuel 7: 23 + 24 NIV

"I will bless those who bless you, And I will curse him who curses you; And in you all the families of the earth shall be blessed." Genesis 12:3 NKJV

Yesterday, 27th January, was **Holocaust Memorial Day,** when the world remembered how Nazi Germany had implemented "The Final Solution"— the goal of which was to exterminate all Jews in Europe – from 1939 to 1945. Tragically, almost 6 million Jewish people died in the Holocaust. To remember this genocide, the UN designated Jan. 27th each year as a remembrance day; this was the date of the liberation of the Nazi concentration camp in Auschwitz-Birkenau, Poland, where 1.1 million people – most of them Jews – had been murdered.

In Israel, less than 170,000 Holocaust survivors are still alive today, and there are survivors in other countries too, each one having terrible stories to tell, of the suffering they went through. Yet there are people who are "Holocaust deniers" who are adamant that this never happened. How absurd! George and I met one of these "survivors" – Rose Price, when she came to speak at the church we attended in Germany, and George interpreted for her.

Rose was born into a strict Orthodox family in Poland. When the Nazis marched in, all the Jews in her village were captured. She endured many types of torture, escaping death several times, and was the only one of her family to survive, spending time in 5 concentration camps.

A deep hatred against Germans and Christians grew in her heart. A Roman Catholic priest in her village used to beat her on the head with his silver cross and call her a "Christ killer", saying that Jesus hated her! In her understanding, she believed that if Hitler, the head of the 'Christian' country of Germany wanted to kill them, then Jesus must be the reason for her suffering. After the war she emigrated to the USA, married and had 4 children, was very active in good works, and became the leader of her Jewish synagogue, although by this time, she had become an atheist, denying the existence of God.

This dramatically changed when one of her daughters and later her husband, were born again, telling her they had found the Jewish Messiah! Rose was furious but went to a meeting with them, where for the first time, she met *real* Christians. She shut herself up in a room for several days to read the Christians' Bible. Jesus revealed himself to her and she also became a *completed* or *Messianic Jew*.

Rose was asked to give her testimony in Berlin, Germany, at the large stadium gathering "Jesus Christ – the hope of the 1980's". As the plane approached the airport, the old hate took hold of her, and she began to panic. She had vowed never to go to Germany or speak German again, and here she was, not just going there, but was about to speak to thousands of these very people! After a great struggle, Rose forgave her tormentors and the German nation, and a great peace entered her heart. When she gave her testimony, there were many tears and people came who asked for forgiveness. God had triumphed and till her passing in 2015, he used her testimony and life to bless many people.

We have met several wonderful Jewish people. One of these was Arie Ben Israel. His family lived in Russia and because they were

Jewish, they were banned to live in Siberia. It was a very terrible time, but when, at 12 years old, Arie's father died in his arms, he whispered a secret to him, *"Arie, Jesus Christ is the Jewish Messiah! But don't tell anybody!"*

Arie was released and went to Israel, living as a strict Orthodox Jew. He and his bride flew to Munich in Germany, for their honeymoon. One day he was walking down the street when he heard singing and people playing guitars. He went nearer and realised it was a group of Christians. Before he could turn away, one of the young women came and spoke to him. He told her he was a Jew and wanted nothing to do with them. The girl's eyes filled with tears and she told him how sorry she was that her nation had caused the Jews such suffering, and asked his forgiveness. Arie spat at her in disgust, and walked away.

But he could not get away from those pleading eyes, and he went into a book shop and asked the assistant to find a book for him about the meaning of Life. She gave him a New Testament! His wife was away for a few hours and as he read and read, he was captured by the figure of Jesus. The Lord revealed himself to Arie as the Messiah, and when his wife came home he told her. His new-found faith was immediately tested, for she said, "You must choose between Jesus or me! *I'll not be married to a Christian!"* Arie chose JESUS!

On their return to Israel they were divorced, and later God led Arie to come to live in Germany. He began to give his testimony and preach in churches, often preaching in the church we attended, and married a German Christian lady. He started an international ministry called *Ruf zur Versoehnung* (*Call to Reconciliation*) between Germany and Israel, and had a very fruitful ministry.

You may think, well, we have moved on since the Holocaust, that's not so important nowadays and it could never happen again. True, it *was* many years ago yet Anti-Semitism is unfortunately alive and well and taking root in many hearts and minds, on the up and up, worldwide. We often hear of anti-Jewish acts of sabotage or hate. Just this week, vandals painted swastikas on the side of a church in the UK, shortly before Holocaust Memorial Day.

The above Bible verses show us that God chose the nation of Israel and made covenants with them, which will last for ever. Our Saviour was born a Jew, from the lineage of King David; right through the Old Testament there are many prophecies about him coming. We as Gentiles have been grafted into the 'vine', not the other way round!

Many Christians and denominations have not realised this, or believe in "Replacement Theology", which says that the Church of Jesus Christ has replaced Israel.

This is unscriptural and God still has a plan for the physical nation of Israel, much of which will be unfolded in the *End Times* in which we are living. We may not agree with every decision their government makes, but as Christians, let's pray for the millions of Israelis, sons and daughters of Abraham, Isaac and Jacob to find Jesus Christ as their Messiah, and as we bless God's Chosen People in any way he shows us -- prayer, financially, visiting The Land -- he will bless us in return!

Prayer: Heavenly Father, God of Abraham, Isaac and Jacob, we would remember your Chosen People at this time. Forgive us when we, or our nation have persecuted Israel in some way. Give us a greater revelation of your heart and love for them, let it spill over into *our* hearts. Thank you for all those who have already found your Son as their Messiah, and we believe you are working by your Holy Spirit in many more. We know from Zechariah 12:10 + 11 that the day will come when "they will look on him whom they have pierced" -- Jesus, the Man with the nail-prints -- and will mourn that they did not recognise him. But Father, by faith, we see multitudes of Israelis accepting him *now* as their personal Messiah!

We pray also for the peace of Jerusalem and the whole of the country, as many rockets and weapons of mass destruction are shot and levelled at them, that your divine hand will bring protection and cause confusion to come to their enemies.

We ask these things in the Name of Jeshua, Jesus Christ, your Son. Amen!

****

Stepping into the New Year with Jesus!

"'For I know the plans I have for you,' declares the LORD, 'plans to prosper you and not to harm you, plans to give you hope and a future.'" Jeremiah 29:11 NIV

This is one of the most powerful Bible verses about new beginnings. The New Year lies before us and is about to dawn! Let's step out today in confidence, based on our King of Kings and His Word, knowing that He will be with us. Faithful as in the Past, so He will be in the Future. His Love is never failing for His Children!

Let's be encouraged today that as we seek His face, we will find our Heavenly Father waiting to show His goodness also to us in this New Year. Let's trust in Him as never before. There will be situations in our lives and in the world, which, if we just looked at them, we would be horrified and dismayed. But with our great and glorious God, you and I will be victorious, and we will plainly see the path we are to tread! *Rejoice, it's better on ahead!*

Let's believe that the answers to prayer we have been waiting for – perhaps for a long time – may be just around the corner, and will materialise in this new year! Our God is a faithful God, the All-Sufficient One, the Alpha and Omega – the Beginning and the End. We have the Greater One living inside of us, in our spirit, and He will put us over! When we need counsel and advice, one of His Names is "Counsellor", and by His Spirit we will be led the right way and receive the answers we are looking for.

For those of you who are going into this new year with a sorrowful heart, because of something or someone you have lost, may the comfort of the Holy Spirit flood and surround you. May you feel the Father's love wrapping round you like a warm blanket on a cold night. He will never leave you or forsake you, and the day will come when He will turn your mourning into dancing, even though it seems impossible now.

One letter, one email, one WhatsApp, one telephone call, one 'chance'-encounter may change the whole of our life, and *God can do this in an instant, for He has been planning it all behind the scenes, usually for a very long time!*

Prayer: Thank you Father, that you have kept us until this moment in time, and that you will not leave us now. Thank you

for the challenge of new beginnings, new ways and new experiences in this new year! We acknowledge you to be the most important One in our life. Help us to strip off of us those things which would hold us back, and to press on ahead with excitement and determination. We reach out to you in a new way for your strength, power and guidance.

Thank you Father, in the Name of Jesus, we receive it right now! Amen.

****

The Butterfly

She walked down the pebble path which led to the lily-pond. Her mother saw her from the window, wondering what caused the questioning look on the childish face. Her short, brown hair falling softly round chubby cheeks, flower-sprigged dress stained from her morning juice, one red sock up and the other down. Life is full of surprises for a four year old!

Suddenly she turned and running back up the path, called loudly, "Mummy, Mummy!" Her mother opened the window.

"What do you want? What have you got in your hand?" The tightly-closed fingers slowly opened; a purplish-coloured chrysallis lay on her hot, little palm.

"Why, a caterpillar has gone to sleep inside there, Sally, and in that chrysallis he will slowly turn into a butterfly! Then when he is quite ready he will come out and fly up into the sunshine."

Sally's brown eyes looked up in disbelief and wonder. "A butterfly? How can he do that?"

"Well, God shows that little caterpillar how to spin the threads around himself and make the chrysallis. Then inside there, he begins to change very slowly into a beautiful butterfly. His old caterpillar skin drops off."

"Ooh!!" Sally squealed in excitement. "Can we see him come out, Mummy?"

"Perhaps. We can put the cocoon here on the window-sill in this little box and every day we'll watch for the butterfly."

So every day Sally and her mother watched and waited. One morning, they noticed excitedly that a small hole had appeared in the cocoon. The creature was preparing to come out! They watched breathlessly, as a tiny head with feelers struggled to break open the hard case and allow the whole body to come through, out of its purple prison.

A short while later, Sally's mother came back to check how the butterfly was progressing, and found Sally sitting on the floor with hot tears dripping onto something in her hand.

"O, Mummy, I have killed him!"

"Why have you killed him? What do you mean?"

"The butterfly! I wanted to help him out and now he's dead!"

Sure enough, Sally's strong little fingers had broken open the cocoon, but the butterfly was dead. The very struggles that he had in coming out of his prison were to make him strong. Unknowingly, Sally had spoiled God's plan. How often God is at work in *our* lives, sometimes shaping us in difficult or painful situations, and instead of allowing him to do his work in us, we try to 'help him out'.

If we would wait in praise, faith and patience, we would see the imprisoning circumstances drop away from us. We would come forth a beautiful person, with stronger spiritual muscles, ready to soar to new heights and experiences in our God. He would lead us to places that we could never have dreamed of as we grubbed along in the dirt like the caterpillar. God has beautiful splashes of colour, perfume and flowers waiting for us -- as we submit to his plan.

Don't be content with cabbage-leaves!

****

The God who leads the Blind!

" I will lead the blind by ways they have not known, along unfamiliar paths I will guide them; I will turn the darkness into light before them and make the rough places smooth. These are the things I will do; I will not forsake them," Isaiah 42:16 NIV

What an enormous blessing it is, to be able to see! So often we take for granted that we have eyes which can see, ears which can hear, a mouth which can speak, and that we have all our faculties! Reading this verse started me thinking about those who cannot see; I cannot imagine what challenges they face, and the enormous courage they so often show!

In a blind person's home, everything must be kept in its appointed place so that they have all they need to hand. Their furniture must not be moved around, but kept a certain way which makes it easier for them to move freely, and not trip or fall. When they go outside, they must be careful they do not get lost or be knocked down.

I was reminded of my father-in-law, Edward Jesze. Edward had Diabetes which caused him to go blind for the latter part of his life. One day, he took his white stick and we went for a walk together. At first, I purposely hung back to watch what he did. Edward walked a few yards down his road, a cul-de-sac. He listened to hear if traffic was coming, then as all was quiet, he crossed to the other side, and I followed. Then he took a certain direction, going down another road, crossing from pavement to pavement, and I was amazed how well he did this. The secret was, he had *often* done this -- he was on a *familiar path,* a way he *knew well.*

This Bible verse tells how God wants to lead those who are blind, and that he will not leave them to struggle on their own but will lead them on those ways which are unfamiliar. He sees their vulnerability and fear, and will lead them tenderly, carefully. One night we were coming home from a service, and were all rejoicing at what the Lord had done that evening. George was parking the car, the children and I were walking down the garden path, and because Emma, Edward's wife wanted to unlock the door, I took his arm. All went well until suddenly there was a bump and Edward cried out -- he had walked into a drain-pipe. I had not been careful enough, not noticing he was getting too close to the wall. He had a big bruise on his temple, but thank God, it had missed his eye being injured! I learnt that it is not so easy to lead the blind as we might think.

Our Heavenly Father would never be so careless as I was. When he leads us, he watches over our every step. Only when we go our own way do we have tumbles and scrapes, and bump into obstacles on Life's journey. Mankind is spiritually blind, and is groping like a blind person, trying to find the way. God even says he will make darkness light before us. When circumstances block and hinder, when all is darkness and we cannot see a hand in front, he will bring us out, upholding us by his strong right arm, bringing us the physical, mental or spiritual sight that we need.

Prayer: Dear Heavenly Father, thank you for these encouraging words, and we claim them today for our lives. In the face of darkness, we speak forth light into our situations, courage and faith to believe you are undertaking! Thank you that you will lead us where we do not know the way, and that you will make the rough places smooth. Thank you for your fantastic promise that YOU WILL NOT FORSAKE US! In the Name of Jesus, we pray, Amen.

****

The Master has come

"... the Master has come, and calleth for thee!" John 11:28b KJV

When we were living in Germany as missionaries, I was working with the world-wide organisation *Women's Aglow* and heard the following incident. A group of *Aglow* ladies went to the yearly German *Kirchentag (Church Day)* in Berlin. As they were setting up their display stand and coffee-bar, a woman popped her head round the corner and said, "Come and see our stand. Perhaps we can work together."

The *Aglow* ladies followed the woman to her stand. In front was a large bush with a snake running through it, with fiery eyes and a forked tongue (not real, of course!), and a large banner with the words: *Brood of vipers!* This was a group of feminists. The *Aglow* ladies quickly assured them that they could *not* work together and returned to their own stand.

Women can be a *brood of vipers,* but they were never intended to be. God is seeking to restore womanhood, dignity, healing and freedom to his daughters today. We were born for such a time and he calls us today to take our place in the plan that he has for us personally and collectively.

The root and motives of our hearts and actions should never be rebellion against men, society and God, as it was with those feminists in Berlin. We will need divine wisdom and discernment, as we step out into new areas. Whether in a career, at home, or in a wider sphere, let's never forget that each of us counts in God's great plan. Together with our Brothers in Christ, we can bring in the end-time harvest that's ripening even now! With humility, yet boldness, let's allow God to prepare us.

When Jesus called Mary she had to leave her house of mourning to run to the Master. If she had not done so, she would never have seen the glory of God in the resurrection of her brother, Lazarus. We too, must leave the negative places where we are sitting.

Let's respond to the Master today!

****

The Miracle of Easter! by George Jesze

"And behold, there was an earthquake; for the angel of the Lord descended from Heaven, and came and rolled back the stone from the door, and sat upon it ... And for fear of him the keepers did shake, and became as dead men. And the angel said to the women, Fear not ye; for I know that ye seek Jesus, which was crucified. He is not here ... he is risen from the dead..." Matthew 28:2, 4, 5, 6 KJV

A Christian man I had known for many years, a church-deacon, announced he did not believe in miracles. I was surprised to hear this, and wondered how long it sometimes takes for the proverbial penny to drop, for he had attended a church where God had answered many prayers, some of which had indeed, been miraculous.

This man was like many Christians nowadays, controlled by their natural thinking, their 5 senses. *Head faith* has taken over from *heart faith.* We cannot understand God with our natural mind, for God is a *spirit*, and as we are made in his image, we are also a *spirit-being.* So believing with our spirit, our heart, is the only biblical way to believe. A 4 year old child can open their heart to Jesus, but a theology professor may reject the New Birth, because he cannot understand it.

This weekend we are celebrating Easter. If we take the miracles out of the Easter story, we are left with only a skeleton but no life. Christianity *began* with miracles! Every part of Jesus' life was miraculous. Today we are privileged to read the *whole* story, but the disciples could only see it in stages. Their understanding was limited, and now, it seemed that the crucifixion of Jesus was the end of it all! *Where do we go from here?!* Their minds grappled with this problem and new situation. They could not grasp that their Lord and Master was now dead. Their world had fallen apart and their dreams lay in ashes.

Of course, Jesus had told them he would rise again, but these words had not registered in their mind. Then, as they were hiding for fear of the Jews and the soldiers, some of their women had come with the tale that they had seen the Lord, and he had spoken with them! Shortly after, two of them ran back from Emmaus, telling how Jesus had met them, as they walked from Jerusalem, with sorrow in their hearts. He had shown from the Scriptures that the Messiah must suffer but that he would rise again, and in the breaking of bread at suppertime, they had recognised him for themselves!

It was miracle upon miracle, and when Jesus came and visited the disciples, they could only stand astonished at his majesty, and stare at the wounds in those hands and feet. He had become **"The Lamb of God, which takes away the sin of the world"**, even as John, the Baptist had foretold, and their lives would never be the same. These miracles may have occurred at Easter, yet their reality will last for all time and every one of us who have made Jesus our Lord and Saviour, has experienced a miracle, **the greatest one of all – the New Birth.**

As David Ben-Gurion, Israel's first Prime Minister said: "Anyone who does not believe in miracles, is not a realist!"

So let's open our heart today for the miraculous resurrected Christ to show his wonders and his love to us in the coming days!

****

The Missing Day or: Restoring the years!!

"The word of the Lord came: Go back and tell Hezekiah... I have heard your prayer and seen your tears; I will heal you...I will add fifteen years to your life...Then the Prophet Isaiah called upon the Lord, and the Lord made the shadow to go back the ten steps it had gone down..." 2 Kings 20: 4, 5, 6, 11 NIV

"Joshua said to the Lord in the presence of Israel: O sun, stand still over Gibeon, O moon, over the valley of Aijalon." The sun stopped in the middle of the sky and delayed going down about a full day." Joshua 10:12b-13 NIV

Last weekend, in the UK, we put the clocks back one hour. As Winter is fast approaching, this now gives us more light in the morning. The downside is, it gets dark already around 5 o'clock in the afternoon! Some of us think it might be better to give us more light in the evenings when we still have activities and things to do! But we have to do as we are told, don't we, and learn to adjust!

Time is very important. Our American friend, the late Harold Hill, businessman, inventor, engineer who worked many times on the NASA Mercury/Gemini series of space launches, told of the necessary ahead-of-time statistical preparation for the moon walk. The space scientists checked the position of the sun, moon and planets, calculating where they would be in 100 and 1000 years from now, also the trajectories of asteroids and meteors to avoid collisions in outer space.

However, the computers ran into problems as they checked in centuries past and the years ahead. **They showed there was a day missing!** The scientists were baffled, then a 'religious fellow' told of a story he had heard in Sunday School, how the Israelite army was fighting a battle against the Amorites. Then their leader, Joshua, commanded the sun and moon to stand still, in order that they might still have time to completely defeat the enemy. God answered him and the Bible says there was never a day like that before or since when the Lord listened to a man. **"Surely, the Lord was fighting for Israel!" v.14. "There's your missing day!" the Christian said.**

Most of the scientists had laughed at this story, but having no other answer, they checked the computers, going all the way back to the time of Joshua, and **found the "missing day"**, but they were **still 40 minutes short.** They needed an answer, for this would have been extremely significant when multiplied many times over in orbits.

Then the Christian came up with another answer, how King Hezekiah was very ill and Isaiah, the prophet, was sent to tell him he was going to die. The king turned his face to the wall, shutting everything out and cried to God in desperation, that he would restore him. God spoke again to Isaiah, that he would answer the king's prayer, healing him and physically adding fifteen more years to his life. Hezekiah asked for a sign that this would come to pass, so **"... Isaiah called upon the Lord, and the Lord made the shadow to go back the ten steps it had gone down..."!**

"Ten steps" means **"ten degrees"** which is **exactly 40 minutes!! Twenty-three hours and twenty minutes accounted for in Joshua's day, then forty minutes in Hezekiah's day – the whole twenty-four hours, the missing day that the space scientists had to make allowances for in the log-book.**

Sometimes we have friends who say the Bible is not true and that Science has the only answer to their questions. Harold used this illustration in his numerous lectures in businesses, universities with engineering students and in Christian meetings, showing that the Bible and Science are not poles apart as we are often led to believe. The God of the Bible is the God of the Universe! I would encourage you to pass on this true story of the "missing day" and pray that hearts will be spoken to, and your friends will look for answers which include this great God and his Son, Jesus Christ.

Now let's apply some truths from these stories to encourage and help us, personally. Two men were in desperate circumstances, Joshua and Hezekiah. Desperate to gain victory for Israel, Joshua had the audacity to tell the sun and the moon to stand still! Hezekiah, who had been an excellent king, serving God for many years, cries out to God to be brought back from certain death, asking for a sign that God would make the shadow go back 10 degrees on the sundial! This was impossible, naturally speaking, but God is the One who made Time and he is a supernatural God; he granted these requests.

I don't know how you are today. Are you in great need, in desperation, crying out to the Lord to bring you answers? Let me encourage you that our great, compassionate Heavenly Father also hears *your* cries, he sees *your* tears. He will not physically turn

back the hours or years, yet mentally, spiritually, in other ways, he can and wants to restore in your life, for he has promised:

"I will restore to you the years that the locust has eaten." Joel 2:25.

Prayer: Heavenly Father, in faith we reach out to you in our desperation today. Thank you for coming and bringing us answers, healing broken hearts, restoring relationships and situations, giving us victory! We acknowledge that you are the only One who can do this; we give you all the praise and the glory! In the Name of Jesus, we pray, Amen!

****

The Old Violin or: The Touch of the Master's Hand!

"And when he has found it, he lays it on his shoulders, rejoicing. And when he comes home, he calls together his friends and his neighbors, saying to them, 'Rejoice with me, for I have found my sheep that was lost.' Just so, I tell you, there will be more joy in heaven over one sinner who repents than over ninety-nine righteous persons who need no repentance." Luke 15:5-7 ESV

"When the righteous cry for help, the Lord hears and delivers them out of all their troubles. The Lord is near to those who are brokenhearted and saves such as are the crushed in spirit." Psalm 34:17-18 ESV

'Twas battered and scarred, and the auctioneer thought it
    hardly worth his while
To waste his time on the old violin but he held it up with a smile.
"What am I bid, good people," he cried, "who starts the bidding for
    me?
"One dollar, one dollar, do I hear two? Two dollars, who makes it
    three?
"Three dollars, once, three dollars twice, going for three." But No,
From the room far back a gray-bearded man came forward
and picked up the bow.
"Then wiping the dust from the old violin and tightening up the
    strings,
He played a melody, pure and sweet, as sweet as an angel sings.

The music ceased and the auctioneer with a voice that was quiet and
    low,
Said: "What am I bid for this old violin?" He held it up with the bow.
"One thousand, one thousand, do I hear two? Two thousand...or three?
Three once, three thousand twice, going and gone!" said he.

The audience cheered, but some of them cried, "We just don't
    understand.
What changed its worth?" Swift came the reply. "The touch of the
    master's hand."
And many a man with life out of tune all battered and bruised with sin
Is auctioned cheap to a thoughtless crowd, much like that old violin.

A mess of pottage, a glass of wine, a game and he travels on.
He's going once, he's going twice, he's going and almost gone.
But the Master comes, and the foolish crowd never can understand,
The worth of a soul and the change that's wrought
By the Touch of the Master's Hand!

Have you ever been to an auction? My father loved going to them, and sometimes he would take me, when I was a small girl. It was so exciting to see what useful, beautiful or unusual object you could buy at a low price, and to hear the bidders trying to outdo each other! But in this poem the violin that was being sold at that auction brings a marvellous lesson to us all. When Myra Brooks Welch wrote that in 1921, I am sure she would be amazed that for decades, countless people all over the world have loved and recited her beautiful poem.

The old, scarred violin is being bidden for a few dollars, but suddenly the scene changes as an old man omes forward and picks up the instrument. Against all expectations, the music he plays is pure and beautiful and the crowd gasps in surprise. The auctioneer jumps in, seizes his opportunity and now holds up the violin and bow, and soon it is sold for *three thousand dollars!* They all asked:

What made the difference? What gave it such worth? – The auctioneer replied it was *the touch of the master's hand!*

So many of us have been like that old violin, perhaps broken and scarred through people's actions, or the difficulties of Life, or just our own bad choices, bound by sin and habits. If we had been sold at a spiritual auction, we couldn't have been worth much at all. But the Master – our Lord Jesus Christ – has come to find us, cleaned us up and started to play his tunes of love and goodness upon our lives. We are now bringing forth a better, purer sound which gladdens his heart, and those around us, bringing glory to God!

Prayer: Lord Jesus, thank you that you are the Great Shepherd, who goes in tender love after the lost sheep; the God who is looking for the broken ones to make them whole. Our life is of inestimable worth in the hands of *our Master!* It is your touch that makes the difference! Today we place ourselves afresh in your hands. Touch us anew with your love and the power of your Holy Spirit, we pray! Amen.

****

The Power of the Name!!

"Therefore God exalted him to the highest place and gave him the name that is above every name, that at the name of Jesus every knee should bow, in heaven and earth and under the earth, and every tongue confess that Jesus Christ is Lord, to the glory of God the Father." Philippians 2:9-11

During the night, and when I woke in the morning, those wonderful words uplifting the Name of JESUS were singing in my spirit. When I turned on a Christian TV program, what song were they singing …? You've guessed it! The Lord must be turning my attention again to the truth of the power in this matchless Name!

It truly does break every stronghold and burns up the dross in our lives like a fire; its light shines through the darkness and renders the enemy powerless; it's the Name to proclaim from the mountains, over our streets, our family – the Holy Name of Jesus Christ our Saviour!

Satan hates the Name of Jesus. There are people who are so bound by the powers of darkness that they can say the word *God*, but they can't speak the word *Jesus*. Satan knows the One who bears that Name broke his power, took the keys of Death and Hell from him, stripping his authority and now all power in Heaven and in Earth is given to this mighty Victor!

I am sure every one of us who have been walking with Jesus for a while have found out how effective this Name is! It's the first Name we call out when in trouble or danger. It was **"Jesus"** my late husband, George, shouted when he was driving a friend's mini-bus, as it skidded on the wet Autobahn, vaulted the barrier in the middle like a horse, then went over the road of oncoming traffic, and down a bank, stopping as a small tree broke its fall. The policeman who came scratched his head in amazement and said George must have had somebody 'up there' looking out for him. He had just come from a similar accident and the car-occupants were terribly injured!

It was **"Jesus"** I shouted when in November 2016 George fell backwards down 8 steps, breaking several bones. Yet how much worse it could have been if he had fallen from the *top* of the stairs, perhaps been killed or paralysed, but God was gracious.

In a book about the life of Smith Wigglesworth – *The Apostle of Faith,* as he was called -- there is an account of six people going to pray for a sick man, who lay in his bed, utterly helpless. He had read a tract about healing and people praying for the sick, and hoped his friends could pray the prayer of faith for him. He was anointed with oil according to James 5:14, but as there was no immediate manifestation of healing, he wept bitterly. The six friends walked out of the room, somewhat crestfallen to see the man lying there, his condition unchanged.

When they were outside, one of them said, "There is one thing we could have done. Let's all go back and try it." So they went back into the house and one man said, "Let us whisper the name of **Jesus**." At first nothing seemed to happen. But as they continued to whisper, **"Jesus! Jesus! Jesus!"** the power of the Holy Spirit began to fall and they saw that God was beginning to work. Joyfully they spoke the Name louder and louder. As they did so the man got up and dressed himself. Those six people had taken their eyes off the sick man, just focusing on the Lord Jesus and their faith grasped the power that there is in his Name!

Prayer: Heavenly Father, thank you for the power and authority in the Name of Jesus! Give us a fresh revelation today of what that Name can do for us and for others in need. Whether we cry it in desperation or can only whisper it in times of weakness and distress, thank you for answering and bringing us the victory! We uplift that Name right now – Jesus Christ, the Son of the Living God! Amen.

****

The Prayer of Jabez

"And Jabez was more honourable than his brethren: and his mother called his name Jabez saying, Because I bare him with sorrow. And Jabez called on the God of Israel, saying, Oh that thou wouldest bless me indeed, and enlarge my coast, and that thine hand might be with me, and that thou wouldest keep me from evil, that it may not grieve me! And God granted him that which he requested." 1 Chronicles 4:9+10 KJV

Nowadays parents often give their children a name which they like the sound of. Yet in Bible times, a child's name usually had a special meaning. Here we read of a man whose mother gave him the name of *Jabez*, as it reminded her of his painful birth. Every birth brings pain, but this must have been an especially difficult one. In the Amplified Bible it says Jabez means "sorrow-maker". I wonder how he felt when his mother looked at or called him – the one who was looked down on? Rejected? Discouraged? The 'sorrow-maker' and 'pain-bringer'? Did he have feelings of guilt, because he had caused his mother so much wounding? Every time she called her son he, and everyone else who heard it, was reminded again of his disgrace. Imagine in Kindergarten (if they had them at that time!), at school or work, everybody would know and perhaps look askance, make fun of him or predict he would have a bad end.

Yet in spite of this bad beginning, verse 9 says he was more "honourable than his brothers". We hear nothing about his siblings. The preceding verses read just like a geneaology and not one name stands out, then come these words about Jabez. What does being "honourable" mean? Probably that he was honest, had integrity, wanted to do what was right, gracious, sought God and not his own way. He could have been bitter or envious, but he was neither of these. Yet Jabez changed his situation? How did this come about?

1. He turned *to* God not *from* Him. When we are in need, downcast or under condemnation, we often run *from* God. But this is the time to turn *to* him with all of our heart!

2. Jabez gave God his full Name – the **God of Israel** – acknowledging that he was the Almighty One who had made

a Covenant with his people Israel, and that he was the God of miracles!

3. He cried out to God in prayer **"Oh!"** This was not just a superficial prayer, but it came from the depths of his being. What did he pray for?

a) He asked for **God's blessing**. Sometimes we make our own plans and then ask God to bless them. Jabez acknowledged that *first of all*, he needed the blessing of God.

b) For **enlargement of his borders**. This would give him more land, increased prosperity and influence.

c) That **God's hand would be with him and upon him.** In the Old Testament, "the hand of the Lord" was one of the descriptions given to the Holy Spirit. Even without knowing it, Jabez was asking for the anointing and power of the Holy Spirit to be with him and upon his life.

d) Protection from evil, harm or pain.

What has this got to do with us? Our mental or emotional condition might not have anything to do with our name, as it was with Jabez; outwardly we may look as though all is fine but we might be hiding inner wounds, fighting rejection, sadness. We may be unwanted, have been abused even sexually abused, been brought up in a broken home, a foster home or an orphange. Our parents may have divorced and the family has been split up, we may be frustrated or bitter at what Life has dealt us. If we were to answer John the Baptist's question, "What do you say about yourself?" what would we say?

The one who never will never amount to anything; no future, the despairing and lonely one ...?

The name of Jacob in the Bible meant a "supplanter, a deceiver", yet God changed his name to "Israel", saying he had power with God and with men, "a Prince". He became the father of 12 sons from whom came the 12 tribes of the nation of Israel.

Gideon, afraid and hiding from the Midianites, was told by the angel, God sees you as "a mighty man of valour", and he became that.

Simon, whom Jesus said was like a reed blown in the wind had his name changed to "Peter" – the "rock" or "the stone out of the great rock". He became a mighty apostle and instrument in the hand of God.

Our beginning in Life is not the most important, but our progress, our goal and where we will end. A few years ago, a friend of mine told me she had just come back from preaching in a church with about 200 people in Moscow, Russia, which was led by a young woman who until 3-4 years before that, had been *a prostitute! Jesus is the great Life-Changer!!*

"And God granted his request"! Such a matter of fact few words, yet for Jabez, his whole life was turned around! **God changed his destiny! It can be the same for you and me too! Many years of quality, joy, fruitfulness, usefulness can be your portion. I want to encourage you today to cry out to this mighty God, just as Jabez did and see *your* situation turned around!**

****

The Saga of the Toilet-Rolls!!

"I will heal their backsliding, I will love them freely..." Hosea 14:4 KJV

This week I was reminded of the true story of a Christian lady in Sweden. I forget her name, so let's call her Ingrid. Some days before, Ingrid had seen a removals-van draw up, and furniture being carried into a house, a few doors down; she wondered who had just moved in. Often when there were new neighbours, she took them a small gift, perhaps a bunch of flowers or a homemade cake, a pretty card with good wishes, to welcome them to the area.

When she was praying one morning, the thought came strongly to her, "Take your new neighbour some toilet-rolls"! She dismissed this, thinking it ludicrous, but this kept coming back to her. In the supermarket, the urging became stronger as she passed the stand with the toilet-rolls! In the end, she bought some and went home. After she had put her shopping away, armed with her unusual gift, Ingrid went and rang the doorbell of the new neighbour.

A lady opened the door and Ingrid said: "Good morning, I'm Ingrid from number so-and-so, and I've brought you a little welcome gift – some toilet-paper!" As she handed the rolls over, the lady's eyes filled with tears. Ingrid felt worse than ever! "Yes, I know it's not what you usually give somebody..." "No, you don't understand. Please come in and I'll explain."

Ingrid was taken into the living-room, and the lady asked, "Please tell me why you are giving me these?" "Well, I'm a born-again Christian, and as I was praying this morning, the Lord spoke to me to bring you some toilet-rolls!" The lady cried even harder, then inviting Ingrid to sit down with a cup of coffee, she told her story.

"I used to be a Christian too, Ingrid, but I stopped following the Lord many years ago. Now we have moved to this new city, I don't know anyone. My husband goes out early in the morning and comes home late at night, and I've been feeling so lonely! This morning I prayed after a long time, and said, 'Lord, if you are still interested in me, show me that today in an unmistakable way.'" She went on, "I went shopping but didn't have enough money to buy some toilet-paper, and now here you are bringing me some! Could this be God's answer, that he is still interested in me, that he'll forgive me?"

"Of course, God will forgive you! He's never lost interest in you and has been seeking to bring you back, even though you were far from him. Would you like to come back to Jesus today?" Ingrid asked. "Oh yes, please!" the neighbour replied and they knelt down by the couch and prayed together. God had done it again! I'm sure the angels had a party at this homecoming! Now the neighbour had a new friend, another Christian to help her and who would introduce her to others and a good church.

Often we ask God to use us and to bless others through us, but we are often discouraged thinking we do not have the gifts or talents which God can use. But let's examine this closer. What 'gifts' or 'talents' did Ingrid use here? I don't think there were any. However, the story shows she had a loving heart which wanted to reach out and bless people. Also, she had obviously learnt how to pray and to hear the voice of God. Although not at first, later she was obedient and did what the Lord told her, even though, at first sight, it could have made her look foolish.

So, be encouraged today, that God can use multiple ways to make us a channel of blessing, even with toilet-rolls! Let's ask him to help us to start thinking 'out-of-the box'. There may be an exciting new assignment waiting just around the corner for you!

Prayer: Heavenly Father, thank you that your love follows each of us, even when we go away from you for years. Truly, you are "...married to the backslider" and will "... heal our backslidings...". And it could be that some of my friends here have not been following you closely for a while, or have allowed things into their life and heart which are taking them away. Draw them close to you today, forgive every sin and give them a new start, set them free from any bondages, and restore unto them the joy of your salvation! We ask this in the Name of Jesus, Amen.

****

There is Hope – for YOU!!

"Weeping may endure for a night but joy comes in the morning." Psalm 30:5

Since the pandemic, much has been said and written about people in depression, or who are having mental or emotional problems. There were many suicides and attempted suicides by people of all ages during lockdown, when the whole world experienced conditions and unprecedented situations and challenges. We have heard of Christians and even pastors of megachurches who have ended their life, and we might ask, "How can this be?! What is the answer?!"

I certainly, do not have all the answers, but this morning it came strongly to me that there may be among my readers, even my friends, people who are struggling with depression and inwardly, there is a great sadness and overwhelming loneliness – things that they have never shared with anyone. Some fall into depression because of great difficulties they are experiencing, others have everything going for them – great family and friends, financially sound, business and job doing well – yet they are being forced into an emotional corner of isolation, trying to hide.

As Christians, when asked how we are, we often put on the "happy, happy mask" and reply "Fine! Fine! Everything's just good!" while inside we might feel like running away or even wonder whether it's still worth living. I heard a well-known preacher describe how he was in a spiritual and emotional wilderness for three years. God was still using him in a mighty way, because of the abiding anointing of the Holy Spirit, but he felt he was dying inside.

One night in his bedroom, he capitulated and cried out for the Lord to step in and change things. Jesus replied, *"I've only been waiting for you to come back to me!"* He fell on his face in gratitude as he had felt that God had left him. He stepped out of the "wilderness" that night. Beginning to put into practice several things he was shown, he never went that way again.

There has often been a stigma about admitting that we might struggle with depression or emotional problems, especially among Christians, or we might glibly say, "Snap out of it! The Lord will help you!" I attended a course given by an Australian minister on overcoming grief and loss. His daughter had suddenly died, just two days after a routine operation. Pastor of a large church, leader of a Bible College, a popular speaker at many events, yet he described his grief and how he did not know which way to turn, after hearing the news.

The people who helped him the least were fellow ministers who bombarded him with Bible verses, and told him it was not right to grieve like that! Those who helped him most were those who sat with him, letting him pour out his heart or they would just sit quietly by his side, or pray as the Spirit led, letting him know he was not alone; there was a compassionate heart, a listening ear, a comforting arm around his shoulder. Each grieving in different ways, his wife and he nearly separated, but God brought them through and a new ministry was born out of this experience, helping people to overcome grief and loss.

I want to encourage you today that THERE IS HOPE and hope for YOU, if you are in depression. Our Bible verse says that although weeping may endure for a night yet JOY comes in the MORNING! The 'night' may last many literal nights, in other words, it will be a 'season' of grief or depression, but God is always a God of HOPE. He will bring us into a 'season' where he will bring fresh joy and dry our tears.

Depression can have many causes, which I am not qualified to teach about. Yet I would like to mention a few things which can cause depression, that I have seen in my life and in the lives of others. God has made us a triune being – spirit, soul and body, and a problem in one part can affect the other parts, e.g. some people have a hormone or chemical imbalance in their body which causes depression and some mental problems, and this can be helped by medication.

Sometimes our life-style needs to change; we may be eating too many processed foods, sugar and fat, and not enough vegetables and fruit. Instead of too much red meat, chicken and fish would be more beneficial to us. Modern farming and methods extract much of the goodness from our foods and we may need certain mineral supplements to make up the deficiencies. Certain medications bring the side-effect of depression. Your doctor may prescribe a different one, if you mention this.

Are we getting enough sleep and exercise? Do we spend too much time in front of the computer, TV or with Social Media? Do we watch pornography or horror films, which are unsuitable for Christians, which bring us into spiritual bondage? There are times when people who suffer from depression need a Christian counsellor. It can be helpful to share and pray together, to find the 'roots' of the problem we may be having, to uncover abuse and rejection which we have denied, and let Jesus into those parts of our life, bringing healing and restoration.

I have often heard that Christians who were earlier in some form of secret society (or their ancestors were), that they need to be set free from that bondage, also to get rid of any regalia or objects they still have. Very often, illnesses or depression in the family comes to an end, when they do this. Wherever Jesus went, when he was on Earth, he brought healing and deliverance to people who were sick or bound by Satan's power. He wants to do the same for us today, if we have been oppressed in any way.

Jesus hears your heart's cry. He sees every tear that you cry, and waits to bring JOY into the 'morning' of your life! There is HOPE FOR YOU TODAY!

****

OVERHEARD IN AN ORCHARD.

SAID the Robin to the Sparrow,
"I should really like to know
Why these anxious human beings
Rush about and worry so."

Said the Sparrow to the Robin,
"Friend, I think that it must be
That they have no Heavenly Father
Such as cares for you and me."

Copyright.   E. Cheney.

Painted by W. E. Mack

Trusting the Heavenly Father

When I was growing up, my mother had a little plaque with the above poem and pictures of a robin and a sparrow on it. The other day I came across this poem again, and would like to share it with you. It has only two verses, yet contains an enormous truth. The birds could not understand why human beings are constantly anxious and rush about, and thought perhaps the reason was that they did not have a Heavenly Father!

In the cares and challenges of Life, it is all too easy to look at circumstances and mountains that face us; it seems we are going down 'dead-end street', with no way out! But nothing could be further from the truth! We have forgotten again that we have a Heavenly Father who daily showers his bountiful care upon us, and has answers and solutions for our problems!

So let me encourage you today, and remind myself, that we can find Peace and Assurance, as we learn to trust this Heavenly Father. If he cares for Nature, birds and animals he has created, how much more will he care for you and me – for we are of more value than them in his sight, as Jesus tells us in these Bible verses: "Behold, the fowls of the air: for they sow not, neither do they reap, nor gather into barns; yet your heavenly Father feedeth them. Are ye not much better than they?...Therefore take no thought, saying what shall we eat? Or What shall we drink? Or, Wherewithal shall we be clothed? (For after all these things do the Gentiles seek:) for your heavenly Father knoweth that ye have need of all these things. But seek ye first the kingdom of God, and his righteousness; and all these things shall be added unto you." Matthew 6:26, 31-33 KJV

****

Truth in the inward parts

**"Behold, You desire truth in the innermost being, And in the hidden part [of my heart] You will make me know wisdom."
Psalm 51:6 The Amplified Bible**

"Behold, you desire truth in the inward parts, and in the hidden part You will make me to know wisdom." NKJV

This morning, these words were resounding in my spirit – **Truth in the inward parts**. When I looked them up, I saw they were from David's Psalm, after he had committed adultery with Bathsheba, and then sent her husband, Uriah, to the hottest part of the battle, to be killed. God sends Nathan the prophet with a message from God to him. David soon realises the greatness of his sin and turns in deep repentance to his God. Here are some more verses from Ps. 51:

1. Have mercy on me, O God, according to Your lovingkindness; According to the greatness of Your compassion blot out my transgressions.

7b. Wash me, and I will be whiter than snow.

10. Create in me a clean heart, O God, and renew a right *and* steadfast spirit within me.

11. Do not cast me away from Your presence and do not take Your Holy Spirit from me.

12. Restore to me the joy of Your salvation.

David realised he had sinned against his God, and cried out for God's mercy and compassion to be shown to his servant. He acknowledged his need for *deep heart cleansing,* to be made "whiter than snow". He pleads for a clean heart and that God would "renew a right spirit" within him, which would be "steadfast" and hold him firm when temptation comes.

Long before he had been made king, David had known the presence of God just as a young teenager, out on the hillsides tending his father's sheep, playing his harp and prophetically singing songs and Psalms. Also during the years of running from King Saul, that presence had kept him steadfast in the midst of great danger. Chosen and anointed by God to be king, this presence was something to be kept at all costs, and now he has compromised it by his sin. He begs that God would not cast him away from his presence, and leave him bereft of the Holy Spirit.

In a completely fresh way, in his repentance, he realised he needed Truth in the innermost parts of his being – his heart, his spirit. He realised that only God's truth would restore the joy of his salvation and be an anchor in the days ahead. He has the assurance that God's truth would bring wisdom into his newly-cleansed heart. Every one of us in our Christian walk have fallen into sin at some time, probably many times. It may not be adultery and murder like David, yet this God of compassion and mercy will also hear *our* cry for cleansing and restoration as we seek him with a repentant heart. Do *we* have Truth in the inward part of our spirit? Is it firmly anchored there or are we satisfied with just a *superficial* understanding of those things which God wants to make an unshakeable part of our being?

Have you lost the joy of your salvation today? Are people and Satan telling you that you have gone too far? God couldn't forgive *these sins you've committed ?!* Has a 'Nathan' been sent to you, and you are bowed down under the weight of his message and your unworthiness? David came out from this through his deep repentance. You and I can do the same.

Let me encourage you today, there is always a new Tomorrow with our God and our compassionate Lord Jesus! David was called "a man after God's own heart". A preacher we once knew, told us "I make many mistakes, but I am quick to repent!" Yes, don't sweep it under the carpet today, but let's allow the searchlight of the Holy Spirit to show the places where we need cleansing and God's Truth to be planted deeply in our heart. We will come into a new stage of victory and strength, and that prized commodity – the Wisdom of God – will be imparted to us in a new way! We will learn to not judge according to what looks right or our culture or the world would tell us, but according to what the eternal Word of God says – **Truth in the inward parts!**

****

Welcome, Holy Spirit!

"And when the Day of Pentecost was fully come, they were all with one accord in one place. And suddenly there came a sound from heaven as of a rushing mighty wind, and it filled all the house where they were sitting. And there appeared unto them cloven tongues like as of fire, and it sat upon each of them. And they were all filled with the Holy Ghost, and began to speak with other tongues, as the Spirit gave them utterance." Acts 2:1-4 KJV

Today, the anniversary of the day when the Spirit of God first descended upon the disciples and all those gathered with them, we give thanks for this tremendous blessing which the Father poured out on them, and that he will do the same for us today, as we welcome him into our lives – the **Day of Pentecost, and the experience of our own personal Pentecost.**

Symbols for the Holy Spirit in the New Testament are:

The Dove, Fire, Oil, Wind, Water, Power

Whatever we might be lacking or struggling with today, the third Person of the Godhead – the Holy Spirit – will come to fill that need.

If we need Peace, he will come as the Dove.

If we need cleansing and deliverance from sin, he will come as the Fire.

If we need physical, mental or spiritual healing, he will come as the Oil and the Balm of Gilead.

If we need spiritual hydration and refreshing, he will come as the Water.

If we need new spiritual breath, he will come as the Wind.

If we need power, he will come with his enabling and release.

When we invited Jesus Christ into our lives as our personal Saviour, when we came to faith in him, he came in by his Holy Spirit and brought about our 'New Birth'. But separate from that is the experience of being **filled with** or **baptised in the Holy Spirit. John the Baptist said about Jesus: He is the Lamb of God who takes away the sin of the world, and he would baptise us with the Holy Ghost and with fire.**

I would encourage you, if you have only experienced Jesus as the "Lamb of God" but not yet as your "baptiser in the Spirit" to reach out for that today. When I was 9 years old I became a Christian and at 14, was baptised in the Holy Spirit, with the evidence of "speaking in tongues". Many changes took place in my life after this experience. It was like having a bigger spiritual 'light-bulb' in my spirit!! I was able to understand the Bible more, I could witness better for Jesus, and the Lord gave me the same dream three times. In this dream I saw myself standing in a church or hall, preaching fluently in the German language. As my second foreign language, I was learning German at school, and the Lord kept bringing German people across my path where I lived in the South of England, so that I was able to learn more. This was the beginning of my call to ministry, especially to German-speaking people.

In the years since, I have been so grateful for the Holy Spirit's indwelling presence and help in so many episodes of Life. The promise is also to YOU! Reach out for it today! Or if you have had this experience and it means little to you now, then I would encourage you to get a new infilling! In the original, we are told to "be being filled" or 'keep being filled' – a constant flow of the Spirit in our lives.

So, I hope you will join me in saying: Welcome, Holy Spirit,

come upon us afresh on this Day of Pentecost, to glorify the Father and the Son in a new way, in our lives!

****

Where shall I go?

"Where shall I go from your Spirit or where shall I flee from your presence? If I ascend up into heaven, you are there; if I make my bed in the depths, behold, you are there. If I ... dwell on the other side of the sea; even there shall your hand lead me, and your right hand shall hold me." Psalm 139:8-10

It is thrilling to me to know that wherever I am in this great world, God knows my whereabouts! On sea or land, travelling by car, ship or aeroplane, in the country or the city, God's presence goes with me. The day will never come when God suddenly exclaims: *"O dear! I've lost Helen! Where can she be?! Angels, we'll have to send out a search-party to find her!"* That would be terrible!

The Psalmist also said that in the light or in darkness, God's eyes still saw him, and it was impossible to flee from him. Almighty God fills the whole universe and makes the earth his footstool. Further, never having seen an ultra-sound picture of a baby in its mother's womb, David could prophetically say that God was aware of the child, with every tiny finger, every fold of skin and developing of the cells and organs.

God is omnipresent; because he is a Spirit, he can be everywhere at the same time. He also knows where you and I are. *He knows our address!* He told Peter three men were coming to meet him, and the address where they should go. He told Ananias where to look for Saul of Tarsus: *"The street called Straight"*.

We heard a true story about a Christian lady in Romania. Her husband, an unbeliever, had left her and their seven children for another woman. Her only financial support was a small amount every month from an organisation in the West, which helps poor families. She was in a desperate situation because she had to pay a large bill and had no money. In her great need she cried out to God, and when the contact person came to visit the family with the sponsor's money, they heard this marvellous moving testimony.

Thousands of kilometres away in America, some Christians had been praying, when God spoke to them about a person in need. He showed them the **exact address and the amount of money needed.** They did not know this lady and knew nothing about the situation, but sent her the money in obedience to God's prompting! How wonderful that God knows our address! Whether our need is money or something else, our Heavenly Father will take care of us. Several years ago when we were living in Germany, our car broke down and there was no money for repairs. Also, we needed help with some literature.

The doorbell rang and two men stood there, whom we did not know. The bearded man took one of our newsletters out of his pocket, saying, "Somebody gave us this and we thought we'd look you up. We're Christians from Manchester and Liverpool. We've been searching for hours. Then someone in a Bank told us where you lived." My husband invited them in, saying, "By the way, what address did you have?" They showed us the address on the newsletter. It was "Postfach 23" (Postbox 23). Not understanding any German, they had been searching for *Postfach Street,* and of course, there wasn't one! God had answered our prayer, for one repaired the car (he just happened to be a car-mechanic!), and they both helped us with the literature.

Yes, God knows our address. He never goes to the wrong house. Let's trust him today and expect his divine intervention on our behalf!

****

Wills and Valentines!

"For His divine power has bestowed on us [absolutely] everything necessary for [a dynamic spiritual] life and godliness, through true *and* personal knowledge of Him who called us by His own glory and excellence." 2 Peter 1:3 Amplified Bible

"In his great mercy he has given us new birth into a living hope through the resurrection of Jesus Christ from the dead, and into an inheritance that can never perish, spoil or fade." 1 Peter 1:3b-4a NIV

Today I was thinking of Wills and Testaments. It's always good to make one if you are older, but also when you're younger! Sometimes people are very happy at what they have inherited, others are furious, thinking they have been swindled or forgotten by the person who died. Many go to Court to contest a Will. We knew someone who did this. A Will can also be humorous. We heard of a man who once left a pair of his trousers to his wife with the note:

"My dear, when I was alive, you were very bossy and wanted to 'wear the trousers', so I've left you a pair of mine!!"

I'm sure she must have been very angry when the solicitor read this out, at the reading of the Will! I don't know if she received anything else as an inheritance!

A Will only comes into force after a person has died, and I heard of something that was very touching. A couple had been married over 40 years and he died in 2017. In the year following his death, on Valentine's Day, a boquet of red roses and lilies was delivered to his wife, with a special card which read: You'll always be my Valentine! Every year since, she has received this beautiful delivery. Before his death, her husband ordered and paid in advance for this to happen. How many years he paid for, I don't know! What a marvellous surprise it must have been for her, and so heart-warming at this imaginative, loving gesture.

In the above Bible verses we read how Jesus through his death and resurrection has bought an inheritance for each person who will take him as their Saviour. This inheritance is being kept in Heaven for us, and one day we will enter into that inheritance of Eternity with him.

However, already while we are here on Earth, he has given us all things that we need for a dynamic spiritual life, because we have got to know him as our Saviour and have answered the call of this glorious, excellent One.

Salvation, a new birth, forgiveness, power to overcome sin, eternal life, guidance, wisdom, protection, healing, deliverance from satan's power, marvellous promises, the Word of God – the Bible, peace of mind, joy, strength in trials ... the list is endless, the inheritance our Saviour has bought for us. His Will is made known to us in his Word. Let's study it and make each blessing our own. How tragic that we often do not know or enter into all that is in our inheritance.

So dear friend, I would like to encourage you to find out what's in the Will for YOU and claim it by faith today, and enter into a new level, a new era of this marvellous life in Jesus!

****

The God who changes "It seems" by George Jesze

"How long will you forget me, O Lord? Forever? How long will You hide Your face from me? How long must I lay up cares within me and have sorrow in my heart day after day? Consider and answer me, O Lord my God; lighten the eyes (of my faith to behold Your face in the pitchlike darkness)…

Lest my enemy say, I have prevailed over him, and those that trouble me rejoice when I am shaken. But I have trusted, leaned on, and been confident in Your mercy and loving-kindness; my heart shall rejoice and be in high spirits in Your salvation, I will sing to the Lord, because He has dealt bountifully with me." Verses from Psalm 13 The Amplified Bible

Lord, I'm really tired of living in defeat, tired of the travail and not bringing forth,
Just drifting along, singing the same old song.
Tired of the words that nobody hears, tired of the strife with the kids and the wife.
Too tired to dream, for it often seems, that you don't care, or remember I'm there!
Too tired to face the piles of bills, Life's crushing pressures and its ills.
From every side, without, within, too tired to start, to even begin.

O Lord, do you care, understand my plight? Do you really care about my fight
Enough to change situations for me, really care intensively?
Do you care enough about my fears, care enough to dry my tears?
Do you see the struggle in my breast, and understand that I need rest?

I am so weary, so depressed, O Lord, can I put you to the test?
It seems when days and nights are long you're a silent spectator looking on.
I'm struggling in so many ways, I'm fighting on through endless days.

O Lord, it seems you don't care at all whether I stand or whether I
fall!

**"How futile are your hopes and dreams!" whispers the devil,
In the time of "it seems".**
How long before will come that day when you'll intervene
And make a way?

**You had your struggles, walked this path too, Lord, it's been
good
Just talking to you!"**

**The very act of unburdening myself has brought me peace,
Has brought me health.**
Your sun is driving the mists away, I see clearer now, see another day!
I see there's victory ahead, I'll worship you, lift up my head,
And tell my feelings how to feel, for the promises of God are real.
**I rise in faith and am on my way with a new assurance, to another
new day,**
**And though my eyes are stained with tears, through the rays of your
sun –**

**A rainbow appears like a prism displaying red, yellow and blue
O I love you, Lord – I worship you!**

**Yes, you've dried my tears with the love of your Son,
So I'll arise and go, and with you run!**

****

"This poor man cried, and the Lord heard (him) and saved him out of all his troubles," Psalm 34:6 KJV

Prayer: Lord Jesus Christ, the Son of the Living God, thank you that you stand with us in our times of distress, in the time of "it seems", that you do not cast us off; that you are the One who will not break a bruised reed but will strengthen it and make it strong!

Thank you for the rainbow of your mercy which extends and glows in the sky of our lives, and reminds us of your greatness and the covenant you will never break. Touch every one of my friends, lift them up and cause them to arise and run to you, run with you, casting off the depression of the enemy, entering into the victory you procured for us on Calvary!

Be glorified in our lives today, we pray! Amen.

****

Worry or the Word?

"But the word of the Lord remains forever." 1 Peter 1:25a NLT

Every Christian must sooner or later make the choice of letting his life and thinking be dominated by *Worry* or the *Word of God.* Let us compare the results of worrying or believing God's Word.

Worry does not bring a solution to our problems. Trust in God's Word points the way out.

Meditating on our problems beings us deeper into failure. Meditating in God's Word brings obedience, prosperity and good success (Joshua 1:8).

Worry has killed thousands, perhaps millions of people. God's Word brings quickening and healing for spirit, soul and body (Ps. 119:50 and Proverbs 4:20-22).

Worry has never made anyone glad. God's Word fills us with joy (Jeremiah 15:16).

Worry causes us to believe fear and the lies of the devil. God's Word produces faith and helps us to believe God (Romans 10:17).

Worry crushes the lonely and drives them to despair. God's Word and the Living Word – Jesus – has been sent to heal the brokenhearted and set the captives free (Luke 4:16-21).

Worry will cause our mind to be clouded with confusion, so we cannot see our way clearly. God's Word will shine upon our path and we shall not stumble (Ps.119:105).

Worry causes us to be taken up with ourselves and the greatness of our problems. God's Word will turn our eyes to the One who is far greater and who is worthy of our worship (Psalm 18:1-3 and 28-30).

Worry will shorten our life. Long life is promised to those who trust and obey their God and his Word (Psalm 91).

Worry is an intruder trying to take up residence in our lives. God's Word should be ruling in our hearts, leaving us no room for this unwelcome guest (Philippians 4:6+7 and Colossians 3:16).

Worry makes us concentrate on our problem. God's Word points us to the solution. (Psalm 119:130).

Worry is a negative force. God's Word is a positive power (Heb.1:3 and John 6:63).

Worry magnifies what the devil is doing. God's Word magnifies how *God* is working (Isaiah 55:8-11).

Worry makes us become introverted. God's Word causes us to look up to him and out to the needs of others (2 Thessalonians 2:15-17).

Worry is a dead-end street. Obedience to God's Word brings us into a glorious future (Deuteronomy 28:1-14).

Worry hinders our usefulness for God. His Word makes us strong and effective (Psalm 1:2-3 and 2 Timothy 3: 16 +17).

Worry is a weapon Satan uses *against us.* God's Word, the Sword of the Spirit will fight *for us* (Hebrews 4:12 and Ephesians 6:17).

Worry leaves us defenceless against the devil's attacks. The Word of God will give us discernment and protection (Proverbs 7:1-5, 24-27).

Worry and fear defile our thoughts, filling us with condemnation. God's Word purifies us (Psalm 119:11 and John 15:3).

Worry is negative seed, which if sown in the heart eventually destroys. God's Word is the positive seed, which if sown in good ground, brings forth life and victory (Psalm 126:6 and Matthew 13:2-23).

Worry weighs us down with unhappiness and depression. Believing God's Word clothes us with a garment of praise (Isaiah 61:3).
Worry does not show us a true picture of the situation. God's Word

acts as a mirror wherein we see things clearly (James 1:22-25).

Worry is temporary. God's Word will stand for ever (Is.40:8 and Matthew 24:35).

Worry brings weakness and inability. The Word of God speaks divine authority and power into our situation (Luke 4:36 and Matthew 8:8).

Worry brings unrest and stress. God's Word brings peace (Psalm 119:165).

Worry will bring us to despair. God's Word offers us a new hope (Ps.119:49,50,147).

Millions of Christians throughout the centuries have proved that using and obeying God's Word instead of allowing worry to dominate their thinking, has completely changed their situation. The late Pastor Yonggi Cho told of one of his church members, who had come for prayer as she had cancer. (He was the pastor of the largest church in the world in Seoul, South Korea; at the time we visited, there were 760,000 members!)

He told her to go home and write 10,000 times "By his stripes I am healed" and read it aloud. The lady went home and took a large pad of paper. She began to write Nr. 1 By his stripes I am healed. Then she read it aloud. Number 2... Hour after hour she sat there writing and speaking, but she knew it was a matter of life or death. At the end of a week she was finished and ran to Pastor Cho with her many sheets of paper, "I'm finished, Pastor! 10,000 times By his stripes I am healed!".

"How's your cancer doing?" he asked. "Oh, I forgot all about it!" she cried. "Why – I must be healed!" and she shouted for joy. The doctor confirmed that she was cancer-free.

What brought about her healing? Her obedience? Her writing? Mind over matter? God healed her because she was more taken up with the Word of God than with her problem. She concentrated on the *solution* and not on her *need.* The Word took root in her heart as never before. Faith was growing and taking over where worry and fear had previously held her in its grip.

God has many ways to heal us. We are not giving this example as a patent recipe for the healing of cancer, but are reporting on this case, which illustrates how God's Word can triumph and bring victory in our lives, over worry and fear.

(Taken from the book *Winning over Worry* **– Chapter 20 - by George and Helen Jesze)**

****

Of Chickens and Sheep or: The God who Answers!

"Casting all your anxieties on him, because he cares for you." 1 Peter 5:7 ESV

"But if God so clothes the grass of the field, which today is alive and tomorrow is thrown into the oven, will he not much more clothe you, O you of little faith? Matthew 6:30 ESV"

Recently I heard Jonathan, a young preacher tell a story about his grandparents. It was when they were very young evangelists and had very few openings for ministry and not much money. One day when the larder was almost bare and not much in their purses, they made known their situation to Jesus, believing that somehow he was going to help them. They then went down to the town and held an open-air at the corner of a street. Grandma played her piano-accordion, they both sang and then Grandad preached to a curious crowd which had gathered.

As they came home and approached their little rented house, they could see a large group of chickens walking down the hill in front of them. They turned in their gate and went into the barn. Grandma and Grandad looked at each other in surprise. The chickens stayed there all night and in the morning, Grandma went into the barn and was amazed to find that each hen had laid an egg – 21 in all! She gathered them up and put them in a basket. Suddenly the hens were on the move and walked up the hill again. Grandma followed to see where they were going and they turned into a farmyard. Grandma went and knocked at the door and a woman answered.

"Hello," Grandma said, "your hens all came into our barn last night and laid a lot of eggs, so I have brought them back to you."

"What?" said the woman, "My husband hates those chickens because they never lay any eggs for us! They must like you, so you keep the eggs!"

Grandma and Grandad were overjoyed at God's provision, and this wasn't the only occasion. Every time they had almost run out of eggs, the chickens came again and laid more eggs for them! After they had lived there for three years, they moved somewhere else. One day, the farmer's wife met Grandma. "Why, you're the egg-lady!" she exclaimed. "Do you know, ever since you have moved out of that house the chickens have never gone down there again, and they don't lay any eggs for us, either!!"

God had cared for his children, speaking to those chickens to bring provision for them! They did not have to feed the hens or clean up after them for they simply came, laid their eggs and left again! What a humorous and marvellous story! We serve a God who can speak to his Creation. He brought the animals, birds and insects to Noah to go into the ark; he caused the big fish to swallow and save Jonah the Prophet from drowning; he put the ram on Mount Moriah so Abraham would have an offering to bring to God instead of his son, Isaac; when Balaam would not listen to the angel's warning, God caused the ass to speak to his disobedient servant ... These are just a few examples where God has shown how he uses animals to fulfil his purposes!

George was in Scotland speaking at a Christian Centre. There was a large area of grass round the building and the lawn-mower had broken down. They had no money to have it repaired, so they prayed for God to help them. That same day some sheep walked up the drive and walked onto the grass. They began to graze, not haphazardly and just anywhere, but they ate from one side to the other, methodically, until all the grass was short and neat again. Then the sheep left and walked off! God had done it again!

I am sure many of you have experienced God's provision, if not with chickens or sheep coming! I know, many times George and I had very little food or money. Once when we lived in Germany as young missionaries, living 'by faith', a Christian man from a nearby village came and dumping a large box of groceries and a 100 German Marks note on the kitchen table, he exclaimed, "There you are then! Please forgive me!" He went on to explain that the Lord had been nudging him to bring us food and money but he had not obeyed. "Then I became ill," he went on, "and while I was lying in bed, the Lord spoke to me, saying 'the Jeszes do not have enough food to eat. How many more times must I tell you?!' So here I am! I'm so sorry!!" Of course we forgave him and thanked him and Jesus so much for this provision. Then there was the time God multiplied the oil in the heating system! The engineer had no explanation that the tank was still so full, although we had had the heating on all the time! There were many other occasions where God stepped in, but that is enough for today.

Perhaps some of *you* are in need today. I want to encourage you that Jesus Christ said he is the same yesterday, today and for ever.

What he has done in the past or for others, he can do for you too! Let's pray together:

Dear Heavenly Father, your Son, our Saviour said that you care for the birds, the flowers, not even a sparrow falls to the ground but that you notice. Yet we, your children are of much more value than them. So today, I bring every one of my friends here to you. I pray your blessing and provision would fall upon them in a mighty way, that you will provide jobs, food, housing, money – unexpected blessing to come over their path. You are the faithful One, who cares for us. Thank you for your help in the past. Thank you for the miracles and answers to prayer, which we will never take for granted. We give you all the praise and glory, and are expectant for your intervention on our behalf ! In the Name of Jesus, we pray, Amen.

****

BIOGRAPHICAL DETAILS OF HELEN JESZE

Helen was born in the South of England. Saved at the age of 9 and after receiving the baptism of the Holy Spirit, she started preaching at 14 years old. God called her to fulltime ministry, and through a recurring dream especially to Europe and German-speaking nations. She learnt German in school. After almost three years in the Continental Office of the T.L.Osborn Evangelistic Association in Birmingham, England, working in the German Department, Helen met her future husband, George Jesze. She moved to German-speaking Switzerland, where George was an ordained minister of the *Swiss Pentecostal Mission*. After their marriage and pastoral work in St. Gallen with its nine branch-works, then in Basel, the Lord led them to return to England, in preparation of a change in their ministry.

In 1974, the Jeszes founded the *Voice of Renewal Intl.*, and ministered in churches and groups of all denominations in UK, Eastern and Western Europe, USA and other countries. They organised itineraries and conferences in Germany, Switzerland and Austria, interpreted (especially George) for many foreign missionaries, had radio broadcasts and appeared on Christian TV programs. They were based in Germany for over thirty years, and in 2016 they moved back to England.

George was born in Poland from German ancestry, and became a British subject after the family's move to England. His knowledge of English, German, Polish and Russian was very useful in interpreting. Having a heart for those persecuted and deprived of the Gospel under Communism, the Jeszes became Trustees in 1999 and worked together with *Eastern European Outreach UK* and their other missions.

The Jeszes' three children are now adults. After 54 years of marriage and ministry together, George went to be with the Lord in April 2020. Helen is now 81 years old, a mother-in-law and grandmother.

Helen also has a ministry to women. She founded and led German *Aglow* groups for 12 years and was active in regional and training activities, and in other women's conferences and meetings. She has a teaching, training and prophetical ministry, also using the songs, poems and music which God has given her. Not a professional singer and having very few piano-lessons as a child, under the anointing of the Holy Spirit, Helen's worship and Psalmist ministry has blessed many in meetings and conferences.

The Jeszes wrote three books (*God's Interpreter, Winning over Worry* and *Born to Win*) which are available in several languages. They co-authored these books together, while Helen did most of the writing. She has written two other books, also produced *Promise of Spring* -- a book of poems and stories in rhyme, and *Devotionals just 4 You !!!* – a book of devotionals with a short selection from George, and preaching and singing CD's and DVD's.

Helen writes online weekly devotionals; her website is www.devotionalsjust4u.co.uk. With a heart for those whose lives have been broken, in her preaching and writing she brings a message of encouragement, restoration and healing for body, soul and spirit and shows how God can enlarge our capacity, creativity and ministry, through the power of his Word and yielding to the flow of his Spirit. She calls us back to our "first love", holiness of living, in the light of our Lord's near return and flows in a prophetic anointing. For 29 years she has been an ordained Minister of the Gospel, holding credentials with *International Gospel Outreach* ministries in England.

I hope you enjoyed reading these poems, stories in rhyme and inspirationals!

Look up my website for more information and to read back numbers of my weekly online devotionals:

www.devotionalsjust4u.co.uk

Books

Devotionals Just 4 YOU!! by Helen Jesze

Winning over Worry by George and Helen Jesze

To contact Helen Jesze, to receive the online devotionals, or to order books,
write to:

devotionalsjust4u@gmail.com